'Marsh exposes the basic problem of the euro: no one's in charge. Monetary union was a colossally risky experiment launched without adequate crisis management precautions and without centralised political oversight. Unlike the other countries, Britain properly analysed the risks and decided, rightly, to stay out. It's a pity that other Europeans didn't show similar caution.'
—Lord (John) McFall, member of the House of Lords Economic Affairs Committee, former chair, House of Commons Treasury Committee

'David Marsh has once again placed his finger on the gaping wounds that continue to afflict the European Monetary Union. While not everyone will agree with his conclusions – and a great many more will hope that he is wrong – he has built a cogent case for being very worried about the future of the single currency.'
—Prof. Michael Burda, School of Business and Economics, Humboldt University of Berlin

'Europe is brilliantly right because it has achieved zero prospect of war, an achievement no other region can match. Yet it's also brilliantly wrong because it has tried to achieve an impossible dream: monetary union without fiscal union. Marsh explains well the European mess and even suggests a solution. His book is a must-read for European policy-makers. Even Asians may learn a lesson or two.'
—Prof. Kishore Mahbubani, dean, Lee Kuan Yew School of Public Policy, National University of Singapore

'A brilliant and incisive analysis of the intractable practical and political problems facing the euro and why the hopes of its founders have been disappointed.'
—Lord (Christopher) Tugendhat, chair, House of Lords EU External Affairs Committee, former European commissioner

'The fate of the euro area is the most momentous public issue of our times and there is no better guide than this gripping, well-informed study by the leading expert on its genesis and development.'
—Prof. William Paterson, honorary professor of German and European politics, Aston Centre for Europe, University of Aston

'This book deserves wide discussion among harried and frustrated policy-makers. I am happy that Marsh has taken up the challenge of discussing a plan to make the euro survive for the longer term. Even though he exaggerates some of the difficulties, this book will have an important impact.'
—Prof. Niels Thygesen, emeritus professor of economics, University of Copenhagen, member of the Delors Committee on Monetary Union

'This precise, elegant, and humorous depiction of Germany's unique role in the euro drama brings the reader to the central argument: without political union, monetary union is left weak or even unviable. A single central bank needs a single political counterparty. Marsh argues that the euro crisis will linger to the point of becoming chronic but rejects the notion of a rapid, dramatic disintegration. It is difficult to imagine a pathway back to national currencies that would not entail even greater catastrophe.'
—Prof. Maria Antonieta Del Tedesco Lins, professor of international relations, University of São Paulo

'A lucid and well-informed, if somewhat German-centric, account of the development of the euro crisis, in which Marsh explains, with admirable clarity, why the crisis has been so difficult to resolve. Although he charts a way out, he makes clear his scepticism that Europe's leaders can deliver on their many promises to reform. Even if he is only half right, pro-Europeans should heed his analysis and warnings, and ask themselves whether the governance changes adopted to date go far enough.'
—Prof. Iain Begg, European Institute, London School of Economics and Political Science

'This book is right to question how the EU can sort out the economic and social mess created by the euro. It is a case of having a bank account with the neighbours before they have worked out who pays all the bills. David Marsh tries to pilot a way through these troubles.'
—John Redwood MP, chair, Conservative Parliamentary Economic Affairs Committee

'An excellent analysis of the crisis in the euro area. The comprehensive diagnosis of the causes of the crisis is accompanied by a sobering prognosis regarding the prospects for its resolution any time soon.'
—Prof. Simon Bulmer, professor of European politics, University of Sheffield

EUROPE'S DEADLOCK

DAVID MARSH is Europe's foremost chronicler of post-war monetary affairs. Managing director and co-founder of the Official Monetary and Financial Institutions Forum (OMFIF), he wrote for the *Financial Times* between 1978 and 1995, including in France and Germany, becoming European editor, and subsequently worked in City financial institutions. He is the author of four acclaimed books on European politics and money, including *The Euro: The Battle for the New Global Currency* (Yale University Press, 2009 and 2011).

EUROPE'S DEADLOCK

How the Euro Crisis Could Be Solved – and Why It *Still* Won't Happen

DAVID MARSH

YALE UNIVERSITY PRESS
NEW HAVEN AND LONDON

For information about this and other Yale University Press publications, please contact:
U.S. Office: sales.press@yale.edu   yalebooks.com
Europe Office: sales@yaleup.co.uk   www.yalebooks.co.uk

Set in Arno Pro by Yale University Press
Printed in Great Britain by Hobbs the Printers Ltd, Totton, Hampshire

Library of Congress Control Number: 2015959999

ISBN 978-0-300-22030-8

A catalogue record for this book is available from the British Library.

10 9 8 7 6 5 4 3 2 1

Contents

Preface to the updated edition

THIS REVISION was completed at the end of November 2015 to take account of changes in the European scene since the book was completed in June 2013. Today's nineteen member states of the economic and monetary union have, it is true, taken some useful and relevant steps towards repairing some of the flaws in the single currency project laid bare by years of crisis, not least the move towards euro area-wide banking supervision with the European Central Bank as the centrepiece. In view of the rising headwinds against more political integration, however, politicians are engaged in a race against time to complete necessary strengthening measures before the next bout of economic unrest surfaces and confronts European governments with a still graver challenge. Despite the undoubted advances in understanding the problems faced by the euro area and taking some sensible structural measures towards resolving them, Europe remains ensnared in a deadlock that is all the more debilitating for having been brought about, above all, by the continent's own shortcomings.

David Marsh
Wimbledon, November 2015

Introduction

History shows us how periods of unstable equilibrium can last a surprisingly long time. During the First World War, the western front was frozen into the terrain for three- and- a- half years. The Cold War between the Soviet Union and the US lasted forty years. For four centuries, Greece was part of the Ottoman Empire. Consequently, we should cherish no false illusions about a quick end to the euro crisis – perhaps all the more so after the drawn-out drama over Greek debt that came to a head in summer 2015.

Europe embarked on the experiment of monetary union in a bid for unity. An associated aim was to render Germany harmless and relatively powerless after German unification and to prevent a return to the old demons that laid waste to Europe in the first half of the twentieth century. After eight years of crisis management since the world was hit by widespread financial upheavals in 2007–08, the European currency saga now pits the creditor countries which have built up large external payments surpluses – led by Germany – against the debtors from the mainly southern peripheral states. Yet, like a spreading disease, Europe's upheavals have transmogrified from mere upsets in the fields of twenty-first-century capitalism and economics into a larger and still more pernicious malady, infecting the continent's psyche and nervous system as well as the body. A combination of debilitating geopolitical circumstances adds up to a powerful threat. Not for nothing did Mark Rutte, the Dutch prime minister, say in November 2015 that the European Union risked collapsing like the Roman Empire.[1] The dossier of danger is indeed lengthy, extending well beyond the state of the currency and ranging from Russian sabre-rattling over Ukraine, the progressively distraught state of war-torn North African and Middle Eastern countries, mass immigration from beyond Europe's borders (which became a torrent in summer 2015) to uncertainty over Britain's referendum on leaving the European Union and terror attacks from the Al-Qaeda and ISIS Middle East movements. As a result, Europe faces the most painful and intensive challenge since the Second World War.

Far from being permanently hamstrung by the loss of the D-Mark and the subsuming of the country's famously independent central bank, the Bundesbank, into the multinational European Central Bank, Germany now wields greater clout over European politics and economics than anyone else. The problem, especially in view of the external storm clouds, is that this apparently strong position makes the Germans highly uncomfortable. Beset still by remorse or misgivings over the last time it flexed its muscles in Europe, Germany has neither desire nor capacity to be Europe's leader. Worse, Chancellor Angela Merkel, leader of the country since 2005 and de facto the strongest leader in Europe, has lost the sure-footedness with which she used to steer Germany, becoming a hostage to the winds of ill-fortune blowing in from all around. This is why, during the course of 2015, the euro, which was already on the way towards becoming an economically weak currency, risked becoming politically weak as well – a trend that looks likely to persist. The myriad trials that Europe has faced in 2014–15, due to both its own economic problems and the effects of wars and conflict on its borders, have underlined the continent's essential rudderlessness, including the challenges posed by Russia's invasion of Crimea, and the response to the wave of migrations from the Middle East, Asia and Africa. Germany, the pivotal country on the continent, has a sense of responsibility, but not of duty. That is one of the main reasons why the euro crisis is unlikely to be resolved. There is a hole in the heart of the currency. No one is in charge.

This book describes how a venture that was intended to improve Europe's internal cohesion and effectiveness and its global leadership credentials for a new millennium has run off the rails. The reasons range from design flaws in the euro system set up in 1999 – flaws that are slowly being corrected – to more fundamental, hardly resoluble problems of incompatibility of different countries' political, economic and industrial cultures. One notable development has been a rise in activism by the European Central Bank, the Frankfurt-based institution that sets monetary policy for the whole of the euro area, which has taken on additional responsibilities, pumped in liquidity to the banking system, and has on numerous occasions rescued politicians from the consequences of their muddled thinking, lack of imagination and straightforward incompetence. Yet the task of permanently fusing national currencies is beyond the abilities of unelected technocrats at a central bank overburdened with challenges, the resolving of which should be the duty of governments. Unless the euro area moves to a more comprehensive system of governance, which is backed by European electorates and acts in their best interests, the single currency bloc will become permanently condemned to deflation and low growth, and the threat will remain potent that it will one day break up.

There are many potentially sensible ways of curing the euro's ills. These range from creating a proper political union for all or some of the present members of the euro bloc, to a peace deal between creditors and debtors, under which the stronger countries pay for the weaker ones. All these ideas have been proposed many times in the past, and they are outlined in this book, particularly in the ten-point plan enumerated in Chapter 20. None seems likely to be enacted with sufficient vigour, perseverance and political sophistication to promote lasting recovery from the imbroglio. Europe, it is often said, has many times drawn back from the brink and emerged victorious from its travails. Yet this time may indeed be different. Not salvation, but a long period of further confusion lies before us – not unlike the inexplicable, unending conflict among Oceania, Eurasia and Eastasia in George Orwell's merciless *Nineteen Eighty-Four*.[2] The debtor versus creditor struggle is one of low-level belligerence between bitter and intransigent adversaries, united only by the certainty that no one will win or even survive unscathed. This is an undeclared war without generals or commanding officers, its course obscured by a welter of obfuscation, propaganda, misinformation, half-truths and lies.

The euro area and its multiple institutions have invested huge financial and political capital to manage the crisis, but not to resolve it. Behind the euro's manifold contradictions lie disparate and divisive forces that make clear-cut outcomes unlikely. We should prepare for neither resounding success nor catastrophic failure, but instead for a further drawn-out phase of standoff, slowdown and stalemate.

1 Unhappy family

NEARLY SEVENTEEN years after the birth of the single currency as a landmark project for political and economic integration, Europe has healed some of the worst imbalances built up during its rollercoaster ride into instability. But the correction from earlier economic overheating has been achieved through widespread austerity that has brought with it recession, hardship and disruption, which in turn place a question mark over European nations' ability to stick together for the rest of the journey. The trans-Atlantic financial crisis of 2007–08 and the worldwide downturn in 2009 exposed fault lines in the euro bloc that had earlier been largely hidden. In late 2015, output among the nineteen members of monetary union was only around 0.4 per cent higher than before the 2009 slump. Yet this masked widespread divergence between the stronger countries like Germany, where the economy has grown by an overall 6 per cent over this period, and the hardest-hit (and previously most imbalanced) states such as Greece, where the economy is down 27 per cent, and Italy, Spain and Portugal, where declines vary between 3 and 7 per cent.

The wastefulness and dislocation of Europe's efforts to curb bloated costs and credit-fuelled speculative booms generated by the single currency have been enormous. Millions of people have had their hopes shattered. Unemployment in late 2015 is 25 per cent of the labour force in Greece, 22 per cent in Spain, 12 per cent in Portugal and Italy, 11 per cent in France and 9 per cent in Ireland – but only 7 per cent in the Netherlands and less than 5 per cent in Germany (slightly higher than non-euro-adherent Britain). Public sector debt across the euro area is around 94 per cent of gross domestic product (economic output), compared with 70 per cent in the early years of the single currency. Although there has been much debate – and some action – about relaxing austerity across the continent to get growth going again, there is still no clear-cut map for the arduous road ahead.

One of the worst outcomes of Europe's malaise is that populations and governments no longer feel in control of their own destiny: in a debilitating transfer of responsibility, shadowy outsiders in Berlin, Frankfurt or Brussels are apportioned blame for national economic ills largely caused by home-made mismanagement. Europe's troubles therefore stem not simply from the dire and divisive state of the economy, but also from vexation and anger about the lack of legitimacy and democratic control in new and ever more complex structures being erected to try to correct these problems.

In theory, a blueprint for breaking out of the single currency impasse is not too difficult to devise. Over many years, the components of the master plan have been the subject of endless academic dissertations, institutional reports, political declarations and government treaties. The list of required elements for success includes a certain amount of harmonisation of economic aspiration, practice and performance; a degree of political and cultural homogeneity; a readiness to share common tasks and give up national decision-making in key fields; and an ability and willingness to steer the overall construct, so that the ensuing combination of costs, risks and benefits is reasonably evenly shared.

Getting this balance right has so far been beyond the capacity of the group of countries, led by France and Germany, that have fused their common destinies within the euro. This is a melancholy band; there are many explanations for their diverse discontentment, exemplifying Tolstoy's dictum expressed in *Anna Karenina*: 'Happy families are all alike; every unhappy family is unhappy in its own way.' The optimists say the depth of discontent opens up a way forward. Citing past episodes when Europe has emerged triumphant from crisis, they argue that vexation is so great that Europe will somehow miraculously forge solutions previously held to be impossible, such as a pact for ironing out debts and credits across the euro bloc or persuading the fearsomely competitive Germans to make life easier for everyone else by increasing production costs and lowering industrial effectiveness. However, all kinds of positive-sounding artefacts to reinforce the euro were proposed in previous periods of relative calm; they were not enacted because no one really wanted them. As a swing in sentiment to populist right-wing parties in national elections across Europe has underlined, crises tend to breed egotism among governments and peoples, not solidarity. Widespread perceptions (such as in today's Europe) that hardship is being spread unfairly make countries more antagonistic, not more level-headed. In most democracies, willingness to put up with difficult and unpopular economic reforms is low enough at the best of times, and can result in the electorate's rejection of the government that proposed or implemented them. When, despite the outward appearance of solidarity in a monetary union, there is no overall agreement on burden-sharing at a higher European level, and when planned European structures seem to lack sufficient democratic control, then the readiness to carry out appropriate policies will decrease still further.

In autumn 2015, Otmar Issing, the German monetary expert who played a vital role in establishing the euro as the first director for economics at the European Central Bank, summed up Europe's dire circumstances – in particular, the obstacles facing the goal of political union:

> Establishing a political union would require amendments to national constitutions and, in most countries, referendums. But voters are far from enthusiastic about the prospect of ceding more authority to Europe.
>
> Initially, monetary union was supposed to propel Europe toward political union. But the euro is no longer a strong common currency that reinforces a shared European identity. On the contrary, it is now a source of deep resentment among European peoples – resentment that, 70 years after the end of the second world war, was supposed to have been eliminated.
>
> To be sure, many have suggested that the current crisis

represents a vital opportunity to overcome these tensions and build an ever-closer union, citing the belief of Jean Monnet, one of the European Union's main architects, that crises are critical to spur progress toward integration. But can this approach work at a time when there is so little trust among member countries? Or would pushing forward under such circumstances create even more resistance?[3]

A vital part in the many-sided politics of the euro is played by the pivotal politician in Europe: the curiously inscrutable figure of German Chancellor Angela Merkel. At the centre of an array of conflicting strains and tensions, she is pulled in different directions by opposing influences. She conveys the impression of rock-like stability, but as the wave of opposition to her immigration policies within her own Christian Democrat party in 2015 showed, Merkel is vulnerable to the changing European tides. Although she is still Europe's pivotal figure, as she reaches over ten years in office she faces a much more difficult power constellation across the continent, with national-minded, go-it-alone politics building momentum in both Western and Eastern Europe, and governments increasingly moving towards policies likely to be inimical to German interests.

Such is the juxtaposition of contrasting forces that Merkel's Law of Permanent Disappointment is persistently on display. According to the familiar pattern of euro politics, seen in numerous controversies over bailout assistance for Greece and in Merkel's tacit acquiescence in the easy money policies of the European Central Bank, Germany's critics habitually call for concessions, which the Germans reject as contravening the euro bloc's tough conditions and invoking the Weimar ghosts of hyperinflation and totalitarianism (a plaintive yet exaggerated contention). Each time, as the pressure builds, the Germans give in; each time, in an increasingly irksome display of brinkmanship, this capitulation comes at a later stage. Yet it is always only a partial surrender that leaves no one satisfied and nothing resolved. The German cave-in is never complete enough to resolve the euro's problems or to win more than grudging acknowledgement from supplicant states pleading poverty. But it nearly always goes too far for Merkel's many critics in Germany, who say she has strayed too far in toning down Germany's rules on monetary stability or in propping up profligate, ungrateful southerners with German taxpayers' money.

One point is clear, although it hardly makes resolution easier: the pain felt by the peripheral euro states is largely their own fault. In Greece, Ireland, Portugal, Spain and Italy, harsh corrective action has been necessary to overcome serious policy mistakes in the euro's early years. Countries used the easier conditions of the single currency to do what people, banks and institutions always do when interest rates are precipitously lowered and then kept low – to live beyond their means. Many euro members built up unsustainable debt in the public or private sectors (or both) that was used to finance speculative economic booms, rather than to generate productive capital investment and lay down foundations for the future.

A subsequent switch towards righting economic imbalances has been necessary and inevitable. But there are three principal difficulties with the outcome. First, sharp falls in domestic demand and rising unemployment in crisis countries have deepened economic downturns and resulted in ever-worsening deflation that, by lowering tax revenues and weakening public finances, have further reduced the ability of states to pay back their debt – a self-perpetuating vicious circle from which weaker states such as Ireland and Spain have struggled for years to escape, and in which Greece remains mired.

Second, in normal cases around the world, where imprudent states incur excess debt that leads to economic overheating, policy rethinking normally leads to a devaluation of the national currency, as part of a bid to achieve greater competitiveness. This is then a component of an overall package of measures to rebuild growth, for example, under the tutelage of the International Monetary Fund (IMF). Under the conditions of monetary union, the path of devaluation is blocked, unless the euro as a whole becomes chronically weak on currency markets (which would probably then further damage confidence) or unless the country concerned takes the ultimate step (for many, still unthinkable) of leaving the monetary union. In 2015, both alternatives were put dramatically on display. The euro fell sharply against the dollar and sterling as the ECB intensified easy money policies to lift sluggish growth and overcome the threat of deflation. And at the height of the summer currency crisis, Wolfgang Schäuble, the German finance minister (and barely disguised rival to Merkel), called on Greece to leave the euro on a 'temporary' basis in order to gain some breathing space in overcoming its economic problems. Mario Draghi, the former Italian central bank chief who became ECB president in November 2011, warned categorically that countries would leave the euro if they found themselves at a disadvantage – a candid warning that broke a long-standing taboo on the discussion of possible euro exits.[4] Statements like Draghi's explain why the sense of crisis in Europe has been deeper than during comparable episodes in the past, and why it is lingering longer. The various euro rescue packages offer hard-hit states and their populations only very long and stony pathways to recovery.

Third, in the case of those euro members where earlier rapid expansion ran aground, there are grave question marks about the governance arrangements that led later to a breakdown in well-being and stability. The economic imbalances in the early years occurred as an intrinsic part of a monetary regime that allowed member states access to easier financing with few questions asked about the outcomes. No one paid sufficient attention to the problems building up below the surface. What appeared to be a supremely benign experience went hideously wrong. Furthermore, nearly everyone bore some responsibility, and this is making attempts to clear up the tangle all the more onerous.

Germany, overall, appeared to benefit. The euro countries that embarked on debt-fuelled expansion absorbed great volumes of German exports. Additionally, throughout the period Germany's currency was kept lower than it would otherwise have been, providing a competitive exchange rate that allowed German companies to prosper thanks to the much-increased exports to the rest of the world. Price competitiveness, together with big increases in Germany's economic flexibility following structural reforms by government and industry, gave fresh impetus to Germany's decades-old capacity to manufacture products that the world wants to buy. As the euro area's largest economy and most important creditor, Germany stands more or less alone in Europe in having circumvented with apparent ease the world financial crisis of 2007–08 and the subsequent downturn.

The Germans therefore face trenchant complaints from debtor countries for allegedly inflicting vindictive deflation on indebted peripheral states, whose earlier behaviour helped (and continues to help) to support German jobs and prosperity. In the eyes of disaffected euro members, Germany not only refuses to take overall responsibility for the skewed state of monetary union, but also adopts an unfair moralising tone in criticising ill-doings of partner countries whose actions it earlier tacitly condoned. One of the euro's objectives was to promote European peace and fraternity. Yet, under the conditions that have emerged, in several southern euro members monetary union has produced defamatory anti-German campaigns of a ferocity not seen since the Second World War.

Angela Merkel has the longest experience and the most solid credibility of current European leaders. Yet she (or her successor) cannot satisfy the oft-expressed desire for some form of overt German leadership to guide the euro area to salvation. This is not just because of the memories of the German bid for domination seven decades ago, but also because of the irreconcilable mix of expectations. The calls of different factions at home and abroad for firm German action – for cancelling part of debtor countries' borrowings, or for agreeing collective European-wide state bonds (so-called eurobonds) so that others can benefit from Germany's credit rating – cancel each other out. For every European who would profit, there is a German who would lose. Gridlock rules. Incessant calls for action from partner countries inevitably run aground on insistent German refusal to give way.

The euro is an overtly political project. This makes still more alarming the shortcomings of the German and European political class in failing to spot the earlier build-up of pressures, and then permanently lagging in the response to the crisis when it broke. The European leaders who, for varying reasons, lent political impetus to monetary union recognised that the monetary union of 1999 was incomplete. One of the biggest impediments is that the European Central Bank, which provides the euro's main operating machinery, lacks a single European political counterparty. Past evidence suggests that something of this nature is needed for a single currency to function smoothly. Monetary unions tend eventually to collapse unless they are embedded in a coherent political framework that allows for effective collective action and burden-sharing, for instance through joint fiscal policy. Many people in many countries affirmed this before and after the euro was born, but very little was done either to prepare for possible problems or to tackle them when they became evident. The euro is haunted by the ghosts of past warnings that were ignored or not taken seriously. Politicians in 2015 put the issue of political union back on the agenda – but there was an uneasy feeling that the rescue effort for the euro project, at a time when the immigration crisis had shown the limits of Europe's internal solidarity, was coming several years too late.

2 Dashed illusions

THE EUROPEAN treaty on monetary union was agreed at
Maastricht in the Netherlands in December 1991 by twelve
government leaders, including Germany's Helmut Kohl, France's
François Mitterrand, Britain's John Major (who secured an opt-
out for Britain) and Italy's Giulio Andreotti. A neat town of
antique shops and multilingual universities on the triple border
between Germany, the Netherlands and Belgium, Maastricht is
an aptly European spot. A still more appropriate venue would
have been Vienna, the birthplace of Sigmund Freud, the father
of psychoanalysis. Certainly, as Angela Merkel likes to say, the
euro is much more than a currency. The motivations behind the
creation of Europe's common money are shot through with a mix
of psychologically complex, sometimes conflicting principles.
Individually, they may sound beguiling; taken together, they
add up to an over-rich combination of desires and objectives
that cannot possibly be fulfilled. Dashed illusions were built
into the script.

During the late 1980s, when, after several previous
aborted starts, monetary union again became a key objective
in Europe, there was no shortage of admonitions against

overloading the single currency project with exaggerated hopes and expectations. Kohl's first finance minister, Gerhard Stoltenberg, warned against planning a successor to the D-Mark for overtly political purposes. Bundesbank President Karl Otto Pöhl scornfully interpreted French moves towards extended European monetary coordination as an attempt to clip the central bank's wings and end what the French called the Germans' monetary hegemony. Prof. Michael Stürmer, one of Germany's most respected historians and a former speech writer for Helmut Kohl, couched his appeal not to expect too much of the euro in terms of Austrian-American economist Joseph Schumpeter's celebrated description of a monetary system being inseparable from the society behind it.[5]

Both before and after the Maastricht summit, the Bundesbank and other central banks in Europe, such as the Bank of England, subjected the single currency plan to searching scrutiny. They concluded, on the basis of experience amassed over several centuries, that an indispensable prerequisite for a successful monetary union in Europe was some kind of political union. Kohl declared on the eve of the Maastricht conference that, without parallel moves towards political unity, monetary union would remain 'a castle in the air'.[6]

More than two decades on, Kohl's words echo with a dull sense of self-evident truth. Constructing political union in Europe was one of four great goals behind the single currency. The sobering reality, seventeen years after the euro's birth, is that not one of these objectives has been fulfilled. In some ways, Europe appears further away than ever from realising them.

Of the four aims, the first and most noble was to promote

rapprochement between the perennial rivals France and Germany, repair the scars of their habitual past wars, and forge the universal fraternity yearned for by the European Community's founders. Political union was not just an end in itself, but a condition for making sure the edifice would not collapse. In fact, the euro house was assembled from the roof downwards: intent on speedy completion, the builders planned to reinforce the foundations later on. However, neither Germany nor France could or can muster the political leadership to move towards a more harmonised Europe combining solidarity with solidity. Although the European Commission, as a result of efforts to repair some of the flaws in the earlier design, has been given greater powers to monitor countries' economic and fiscal policies, no country is willing substantially to transfer sovereignty to other nations, for fear that the costs could outweigh the benefits.

The second aim was to provide the wherewithal for cross-border trade and investment under the European single market championed in the 1990s by European Commission President Jacques Delors (backed by a variety of European politicians, including Margaret Thatcher). Delors' doctrine was that, without a single currency, Europe's market would be incomplete and its citizens would be materially poorer. But in the past ten years, slow growth in Europe has put a powerful damper on internal trade. The major markets of the future lie outside monetary union: it is with non-euro countries – in Asia, Latin America, Central and Eastern Europe – that euro members' trade has burgeoned. As of 2012, the proportion of total German trade (goods exports and imports) within monetary union was down to 38 per cent (from 46 per cent in 1999, when the euro was introduced). For France, the percentage had fallen from 52 per cent to 47 per cent; for Italy, from 53 per cent to 42 per cent; for the Netherlands, from 55 per cent to 49 per cent; and for Spain, from 59 per cent to 45 per cent. The main reason prompting trade with countries outside the euro is their economic dynamism; it has nothing to do with exchange rates, since all these non-euro states have currencies that float against the euro. A common currency is neither a necessary nor a sufficient condition for an effective common market.

Third, both the French and the Germans, for different reasons, wished to set up a new European currency that would challenge the monopoly power of the dollar. The French wanted this because they had long been jealous of the so-called US 'exorbitant privilege': America's ability to issue virtually unlimited volumes of dollars that provide an easy way of financing budgetary and payments deficits. The Germans took a more moralising approach, wishing to exert discipline on unbridled US monetary and fiscal policies and so promote world financial stability. Very little of this worked out as planned. Deficit spending continued in the US for some years, and was one of the causes of the 2007–08 upheavals, but it was the Europeans, not the Americans, who led the world in waywardness. By setting up a currency that became the No.2 reserve asset after the dollar, the Europeans attracted substantial footloose international capital into the euro area, at interest rates that were far too low, considering the risks the creditors were taking on. This capital went to finance speculation-induced private and public indebtedness in problem countries

– indebtedness that became unsustainable. In recent years, the euro's problems have caused it to lose ground in popularity as a reserve asset. Bolstered by America's geopolitical power, the depth and breadth of US financial markets and America's much more buoyant recovery from recession, the dollar remains by far the world's dominant currency.

The fourth Maastricht aim is the most psychologically fraught: to curb the power of reunified Germany by replacing the Bundesbank with the European Central Bank and by subsuming the D-Mark under the euro. Two decades on, other European efforts to dilute the might of Germany have failed, just as the Germans have seen their own hopes dashed – hopes of using the euro as a shield in their bid to avoid greater responsibility in international affairs. Germany's position in European politics and economics is at a post-war high. But precisely because this strength touches off irritation and jealousy among neighbouring countries, the Germans remain massively vulnerable.

France's expectation that the single currency would snuff out Germany's aggressive vitality was always likely to turn out an expensive error. Shortly before his death in January 1996, François Mitterrand confessed that handing over management of European money to a German-style independent central bank had been a miscalculation, for which he could no longer make amends. Gerhard Schröder, Merkel's predecessor as German chancellor between 1998 and 2005, summed up the results: 'If France's political aim was to create the euro as part of a plan to weaken Germany so as to reduce our supposed economic dominance, then the result has been exactly the opposite.'[7] Schröder's declaration of victory was all the more convincing because, back in 1998, he had predicted that the euro would end up enhancing Germany's competitiveness, and thus not weakening but strengthening his country against its European neighbours.

France's misfortune after 1999 was to react in exactly the opposite way to Germany to the challenges of an increasingly competitive world. In the 1990s, the French had launched successful policies of disinflation, while Germany under Kohl failed to take the necessary post-unification reforms. So France entered monetary union with a better-performing economy. After 1999, the tables were turned: the Germans under Schröder brought in heavyweight economic restructuring, while the French rested on their laurels. This resulted in an increasingly wide gap between the economic leaders and the also-rans in Europe. Germany's string of payments surpluses against the debtor countries in Europe ended up with the Germans amassing €1,000 billion in net foreign assets – claims on Europe and the rest of the world that the Germans will be anxious to defend in any further European debt restructuring. The euro has led to a widening gap in industrial modernisation between Germany and other leading creditor economies in Northern Europe and the debt-ridden southern countries. This is an unstable state of affairs, for it is hardly credible that the creditor countries, led by Germany, will wish to take action to sustain indefinitely debtor countries that are becoming less solvent, more querulous and less relevant. Germany's greatly expanded financial claims give the Germans the appearance of strength. They, however, believe that they are more susceptible to setbacks than many people think, since a sizeable proportion of the debts will never be repaid – graphically shown from 2015 onwards by the protracted wrangle over rescheduling Greece's huge and fundamentally unpayable debts. A pattern of light and shade mixed with misperception: a metaphor for a confused continent.

3 The German question revisited

THE EURO'S establishment formed part of decades-old efforts to resolve the 'German question'. Cutting the newly reunited Germans down to size was an aspiration with which leading Germans readily concurred, because they wished to integrate Germany's new potency within a genuinely European framework. Helmut Kohl famously said that Germany had no interests of its own, since they were always aligned with those of Europe. He agreed wholeheartedly when François Mitterrand declared that 'more Germany' had to be countered by 'more Europe'. But the awkward role of Europe's pivotal nation – as historians have stated, too big to fit neatly into the balance of power, yet too small to impose a new hegemony[8] – remains a source of mystery and agitation both for neighbouring countries and for the Germans themselves. The result is political confusion and perfectly balanced indecision.

After a difficult earlier period of adjustment, in which Germany appeared to be struggling amid the persistent shockwaves of reunification, monetary union eventually contributed to a German renaissance by strengthening further the mainspring of the country's post-war recovery: exports. Germany seems to be assuming a leadership role in European economics and politics; but for primarily historical reasons it is extremely wary of acknowledging the fact and of accepting the role, to say nothing of engaging constructively with the idea and turning it into a success. Since the Second World War, Germany has followed European policies that simultaneously promoted stability and expansion in Germany and the rest of Europe. Now, for the first time for decades, competing European and domestic priorities are pushing the country in different directions.

Over the past ten to fifteen years, German economic policy has been much more successful than in most other countries. Germany has become a benchmark for other nations – rightly so. Yet the guiding principle of European cooperation has been to escape a 'German Europe' by establishing a 'European Germany'. The Europe that looks set to emerge economically in coming years is likely to be a Europe based on the German model. This engenders opposition and resentment from non-Germans anxious about a revival of old demons, and unease from the Germans at the thwarting of their own planned self-emasculation.

Former German Chancellor Helmut Schmidt's description of Germany as an economic giant but political dwarf is still applicable; the Germans on the whole prefer to stay pygmies. Or, as Heinrich Heine described his countrymen's state of mind almost two centuries ago: 'Like boys we want to run off daily into the wide world. But when at last we really are in the wide world, we find it too wide, and often secretly yearn for the narrow stupidities and wrong things at home, and would like to sit between the old familiar walls.'[9]

In the long run, Europe is likely to be split between those countries that are economically and politically compatible with Germany, and those that are not. Germany appears to be willing to follow a common path towards fiscal and political union only with the other creditor nations that share similar economic cultures and experiences, such as the Benelux countries or Austria. The paradox is that the sole states with which it is willing to forge genuine union are those that have no need of it. The debtor countries in the southern part of the continent require fiscal transfers and political union, but Germany would accept them only if they cease to be debtors – and no longer need the money. Yet Germany will not take direct steps to implement any kind of selection process for countries capable of sustaining euro membership. Separating the wheat from the chaff would be too robust an exercise for modern-day Germans. They might accept a lengthy, messy, laborious self-selection process under which the neighbouring countries decide for themselves whether or not to stay in a more tightly bound euro area. The one stipulation the Germans would make is that they would not be liable for the consequences.

The old European nations, Britain and France, with centuries of practice in running strategic initiatives in pursuit of their own interests, would like to continue those traditions, but are stymied in this by economic weakness. Germany has the economic wherewithal to develop its own strategy, but lacks the necessary self-confidence, expertise and experience to realise this goal. To paraphrase US Secretary of State Dean Acheson's reference to post-Second World War Britain: upon unification Germany recovered its sovereignty, but has not yet found a role.

Other nations treat Germany and its post-war achievements with respect, mixed with a certain hesitancy: over the past century, the Germans have, after all, been both too bad, and too good, to be true.

Another factor compounds the qualms: all too often, lacking empathy to put themselves in the position of their neighbours, the Germans have a tendency to make moralising judgements about what other euro members should or should not do. On the other hand, in the early years of monetary union, when reckless credit expansion and rising economic imbalances in Europe were storing up grave financial problems, the Germans, with their own problems to overcome, simply did not notice. When bad times broke out, the Germans overlooked the fact that their relentless insistence on deflationary orthodoxy for their neighbours (even if the policies were necessary to overcome self-inflicted short-comings) carried connotations of neo-colonialism or worse.

However, this is a psychological trap from which there is little hope of escape. Among the solutions for the euro's mishaps, logical analysis might suggest that Germany should simply leave the currency club, accompanied by other like-minded neighbours, such as the Netherlands, Luxembourg and Austria. They would then form a cohesive 'northern euro' bloc of creditor countries with exchange rates and interest rates more suited to their needs. The southern countries, whose economies proceed to a different rhythm, would form their own grouping. The big question would be what to do about France – since the Second World War, Germany's staunchest ally on the continent – which in recent years has been moving economically in a different direction from Germany.

The European economy as a whole might well be more stable as a result of splitting the euro. A policy of break-up was put forward by a new anti-euro political party founded to fight the 2013 German general election, Alternative for Germany (AfD). Although the party just failed to win enough votes to enter parliament, it is being taken seriously by Merkel and her allies. The anti-euro group has shifted popular German debate towards a more unbending stance on aid for problem-hit euro members. Both the AfD and other anti-establishment parties gained strength in Germany in 2015 as, despite the undeniable benefits the euro had brought to the country's export industry and the many millions of workers in that sector, popular suspicion about the euro, alongside unease over immigration, fused together in support for right-wing populists opposed to more European integration. But the AfD is likely to be of no more than nuisance value. The route it advocates is blocked. As the leading progenitor of the euro project, Germany cannot simply pull out.

With unification in 1990, Germany regained its sovereignty but not its manoeuvrability. The political and economic consequences of deserting the European mainstream, reversing sixty years of post-war foreign policy, would be earth-shattering. On the other hand, Germany finds the alternative increasingly distasteful: permanent exposure to blackmail from other member states seeking financial inducements to preserve the euro club. The growing influence of anti-euro commentators and groupings in Germany will further harden public opinion against sending southwards more German taxpayer support. But for the Germans, leaving the euro cannot be an option.

For equal and opposite reasons, the weaker euro countries have little incentive to leave the euro bloc, though they would benefit from a more competitive exchange rate and a relaxation of the fierce austerity programmes brought in as the price to pay for various bailout actions. Their departure would cut them off from large-scale sources of financing and expose them to an uncertain future. Germany and other creditor countries may wish others to leave, but they cannot force them out. The fear is that, if Greece were to quit the single currency, it would destabilise the entirety of Europe – not only by generating economic chaos, but also by creating conditions that might encourage further mass migration to northern Europe, as well as potentially creating a breeding ground that might be infiltrated by terrorist groups linked to Europe's troubled peripheral border regions in the 'arc of crisis' stretching from Ukraine to North Africa and the Middle East. So however fervently many Germans (including Wolfgang Schäuble, the finance minister) wished Greece to leave the euro in 2015, the influences binding the Greeks to it paradoxically became all the more powerful. The creditor countries have also made it clear that if members do exit the euro, the experience should be painful in the extreme for the departing country, so as to discourage others from following suit. The array of barriers to euro exit represents a recipe for political paralysis of the most insidious kind.

4 Winners and losers

THE GLOOMY predictions of the late German-British sociologist Ralf Dahrendorf, who said that the euro would split rather than unite Europe, have become a reality. The gap between creditors and debtors has become unbridgeable. The former are disconcerted or outraged by flows of funds to help hard-up southern Europe, viewing this as unfairly rewarding failing countries and as breaching the celebrated 'no-bailout' clause of the Maastricht treaty. The latter are full of resentment about the painful recessions now spreading around the Mediterranean and beyond: they blame the northern creditors for engineering austerity and depression to force southern countries to reduce consumption and ensure repayment of their invested capital. Europe is a place of winners and losers. Alongside its own money, the continent has built up its own brand of conspiracy theories.

All this makes it increasingly unlikely that the two sides can find solutions geared to safeguarding each other's mutual interests. Europe is becoming fractured – not simply by assets and liabilities, but also by hard-to-reverse differences in the industrial landscape, as modern high-tech industry, investment and employment become increasingly concentrated around the economic core of Germany and nearby states.

Countries on the receiving end of painful realities cannot say they were not warned. A host of leading figures told would-be member states at the end of the 1990s that joining monetary union would be the easy part, and that strife could follow. In contrast to European politicians' assertions that the euro would serve peace, Harvard economist Martin Feldstein predicted that it could lead to conflict. Hans Tietmeyer, Bundesbank president in the years before the single currency was launched in 1999, warned repeatedly of the threat of disintegration for a monetary union composed of sovereign states that were not linked by political union. He stated that countries that could no longer devalue would have to show flexibility in other economic fields to avoid higher unemployment:

> A country with insufficient convergence could quickly reach the limits of its adaptability. Necessary severe cuts in the labour market or in the area of public finances would weigh heavily on the acceptance of the euro in this country, not to mention the burdens for other members in capital market interest rates and potential conflicts between [member] countries.[10]

This cautionary advice went unheeded. Countries fixed their nominal exchange rates by eliminating national currencies; but costs and productivity continued to diverge, dividing individual members of the euro bloc into two categories in the early years of monetary union. Both groups of countries faced what appeared to be the same set of monetary parameters; but in reality, allowing for the widely disparate structures and circumstances of the individual nations, the conditions were radically different. In the first camp were countries with low growth and low inflation, led by Germany, where domestic economic expansion was held back by what was perceived as relatively high interest rates at the European Central Bank. These euro members rapidly gained in competitiveness and shifted more resources into the export sector, to compensate for economic sluggishness at home. In the second camp were the more inflation-prone countries with initially higher growth rates: the less advanced members from the south and west of the euro area, which saw the single currency as a chance to catch up with their richer brethren in the north. This category was in a totally different environment, since the ECB's unified monetary policy confronted them with interest rates that were in fact too low, leading to progressive domestic overheating and reduced exports caused by declining competitiveness.

Although nominal exchange rates within Europe were stable (since the euro's predecessor currencies had been abolished), the real exchange rates (allowing for sharp cost differences between the individual members) diverged widely. At first, everything went well. Sharply higher balance of payments surpluses and deficits were financed more or less automatically. In a form of vendor finance, the countries with export surpluses simply built up financial claims on the progressively more indebted nations with growing trade deficits. Monetary union seemed to be producing a satisfactory degree of European interdependence. The foreign assets of the first group increased steadily, as did the international liabilities of the second category – and with this came increased mutual financial vulnerability. But after the September 2008 collapse of US investment bank Lehman Brothers ushered in the financial crisis, this vulnerability slowly became more acute. Large proportions of the sizeably higher liabilities in Greece, Portugal and Spain were financed by short-term cash flows, which are notoriously fickle at times of upheaval. The willingness of the creditor countries to pump funds into the deficit nations at low interest rates started to tail off – and then dropped precipitously as creditors all sought together to pull their funds out.

By 2009, the European Commission calculated that, if national exchange rates had still been in existence, the Spanish peseta, Portuguese escudo and Greek drachma would have had to depreciate by 10 to 15 per cent, and the German D-Mark would have needed to revalue by a similar amount. On account of different European labour and production costs, countries at different ends of the competitiveness scale had built up a real divergence of 30 per cent. The combined results of the real (inflation-adjusted) devaluation of the 'German euro' and the real appreciation of the Spanish, Portuguese and Greek versions of the single European currency were devastating: the more competitive group of countries in core Europe, led by Germany and the Netherlands, built up increasing trade surpluses, while the higher-cost peripheral countries (including Italy, Portugal, Spain, Greece and Ireland) suffered widening deficits.

As investors' risk aversion increased from its previous low ebb, creditor nations became aware that they could face losses from actual or potential default by borrowers. A vicious circle set in, with interest rates on indebted countries' government bonds rising inexorably, leading to progressive difficulty in attracting new loans and greater fragmentation of European financial markets – the opposite of what the progenitors of monetary union had intended. As private sector creditors withdrew, rapid changes in financial conditions, worsening of banks' positions and the flight of capital from debtor countries raised the need for official intervention from official lenders – the so-called 'troika' of the IMF, the European Union and the ECB – to prevent defaults in the abruptly exposed peripheral countries. Greece, Ireland, Portugal, Spain and Cyprus all had to submit to austerity packages as the condition for rescue operations – a powerful setback for any hopes that Europe could overcome its challenges without violent contortions.

Punctured dreams were pre-programmed. Prof. Wilhelm Nölling, a Hamburg economist and politician who was a member of the Bundesbank's policy council until 1992, wrote in 1993 that monetary union would be a 'straitjacket' that should only be imposed on countries that no longer needed exchange rate adjustments as an instrument of economic policy.[11] One of the obdurate German professors who, for over two decades, have mounted constant legal actions against the euro, Nölling foresaw that members of monetary union 'would channel their finances into improving their own competitiveness rather than helping the backward elements. Monetary union maps out a retreat from solidarity.' Nölling's prophecy proved accurate. A common currency has divided the continent.

5 A dangerous vacuum

THE EURO has turned out to be a currency for which nobody is responsible. Although it is apparently run by an independent European Central Bank, no fully fledged political European entity is really in charge. Instead, management is in the hands of a cacophonous collection of European states attempting to combine as much control as necessary with as many elements of national sovereignty and self-determination as possible. This is one of the main reasons why the euro is and will remain in limbo. In monetary union's positive early years, leaders queued up to claim credit for the euro's perceived successes. Once the sovereign debt crisis came to a head, the euro found itself bereft of friends and protectors. Instead, all the actors in the saga rushed to blame each other for newly manifest shortcomings.

From the beginning, the euro's advocates described it as 'denationalised money'. Its value would be upheld by a European Central Bank reassuringly free of government influence, along the lines of the successful German Bundesbank. But it was always a mistake to assume that the Bundesbank's supposedly transformative might could be seamlessly transferred, as if by conjuring trick, to the rest of Europe. The powers of a central bank, however independent, are always limited. They apply to such operational areas as controlling the money supply and providing bank liquidity. These are ultimately technical, not political functions; and there is certainly nothing magical about them. A sustainable currency requires far more than a technically efficient central bank. It needs to be embedded in a constitutional framework governing the separation of powers between the government and central bank that can stand the test of time.

The fiction of a regenerative single currency driven by an all-powerful monetary body was propagated equally fiercely by both proponents and opponents of independent central banks. Some, especially in Germany, wanted to make the ECB's immunity from political interference the keystone of the new European architecture. Others, led by the French, wanted to channel the Bundesbank's supposed strength into a new order, where the prestige and dignity of the German bank that ruled Europe's money could serve Europe's wider interests. From the beginning, monetary union was imbued with a metaphysical touch; hope was borne aloft that it would fuse many nations with proud and disparate histories into a benevolently united force.

No man better personified this soaring idealism than Jean-Claude Trichet, a self-confident French economic technocrat, seemingly born for the duties he eventually discharged for eight years, with theatrical aplomb, as president of the European Central Bank. In the early, relatively smooth-running period, Trichet periodically irritated finance ministers by suggesting he should be designated 'Mr Euro' in order to affirm his bank's freedom from political control. In the subsequent years of grinding attrition, during endless crisis meetings, that was not an accolade anyone was particularly anxious to claim.

Trichet's moment of hubris came in June 2008, at a ceremony in Frankfurt's ceremonial opera house to celebrate the tenth anniversary of the ECB. He hailed the euro as 'a remarkable success' and grandiloquently declared that he had no wish 'to name and shame' those who predicted it would fail.[12] Pride goes before a fall. In the period after summer 2008, the inherent limitations of the new central banking system became apparent. With growing frustration, many peripheral countries realised that the ECB – a multinational complex with no real controlling core, many national shareholders with different views, and no centralised fiscal counterparty – was bereft of important powers that could be vital in a crisis. In particular, in contrast to the US Federal Reserve, the Bank of Japan or the Bank of England, during the tense early years of the financial crisis the ECB could not act to regulate liquidity and interest rates on the capital markets by making large-scale purchases of government bonds, using the practice which (for the other central banks) became known as 'quantitative easing'. This was partly because there was no accord on which countries' debt instruments should be acquired in this way, and also because some countries (especially Germany) believed that such intervention would infringe the European treaty prohibition on monetary financing of deficits. Germany reluctantly relaxed its strictures on quantitative easing only years later, allowing large-scale ECB government bond purchases to get under way only as late as March 2015, in reaction to a sharp fall in inflation to well below the central bank's mandated target of below-but-close-to 2 per cent.

A further constraint on the operation of monetary union became apparent only after the financial turbulence. The bloc's members had exchanged their national currencies for the euro. Yet few realised that the new monetary unit was in fact a foreign currency, beyond the control of the respective nation – in fact, a currency beyond the direct control of any entity whatsoever. Specifically, governments issuing debt in the new currency became entrapped. Although there was an important advantage, in that borrowing was at a lower interest rate than in the past, a significant risk was attached: normally, when governments borrow in their own currency, they can influence the currency in their favour, but now there was no opportunity for this. Issuing debt in what was effectively a foreign currency could end up an extremely expensive luxury. Although some of the euro's early technical architects were aware of this potential hazard and thought it would help impose monetary discipline, the politicians did not spot the trap until much later.

Guillermo de la Dehesa, an experienced Spanish monetary official and veteran of various stages of the euro drama, summarises the pitfalls:

Countries that join a monetary union lose more than one instrument of monetary policy. They also lose their capacity to issue debt in a currency over which they have full control, so that they issue debt in a kind of foreign currency. For instance, if Spain tries to sell bonds to investors who start to fear its potential default, then it has to pay much higher interest rates. The Spanish government can no longer ask or force the Bank of Spain to buy government debt because it does not control that institution. It cannot ask for liquidity from the ECB because it is forbidden by the [European treaties]. Therefore, it suffers a liquidity crisis; that is, it cannot obtain funds to roll over its debt at reasonable interest rates. Investors see that their fears become a reality, and a self-fulfilling crisis starts until a potential default becomes a reality.[13]

Because of the absence of a political union and a European state system, and because of the ECB's own limitations, members of monetary union are exposed to a dangerous vacuum that can fatally undermine its operation. At the time of the euro's foundation, no member state fully realised that single monetary policy paves the way for economic distortions of hugely destructive potential, with no capacity for resolution by any single decision-making entity. Because no one can exert real leverage over the outcome, the various pockets of economic and political power – whether in Brussels, Berlin, Frankfurt or Paris – are frequently occupied in squabbling and shifting blame, rather than in banding together in genuine collective action. The economic processes unleashed by monetary union are in some ways reminiscent of the automatic functioning of the nineteenth-century Gold Standard or of the late twentieth-century European exchange rate mechanism, where the weaker countries' initial benefits are eventually dissipated by submission to conditions imposed by the stronger states. Yet there is an important difference. The setbacks suffered by the countries in difficulties from being tied to an exchange rate and interest rates that do not match their needs are serious enough. But the hurdles they would face if they tried to leave the euro are incomparably larger than those confronting states in similar positions which sought withdrawal from previous monetary arrangements. The sole available route stretches out further across the quicksand.

6 Irreparable errors

A PROCESSION of design flaws and implementation errors has become ingrained in the fabric of monetary union. The shortcomings were obscured for a while by the euro's relatively problem-free technical introduction, enlargement of the euro area to include additional countries (led by Greece in 2001) and the initially successful adaptation to the trans-Atlantic financial crisis. However, since intractable difficulties started to break out, led by the 2010 Greek imbroglio, the euro's operating mechanisms have been progressively deformed through a range of support and intervention measures, assembled usually through laborious compromises of ever greater complexity. The euro is being shored up by complex contrivances for artificial life support. The battery of rescue procedures, described with inscrutable technical acronyms, represents a significant reversal from the euro's original ideals of a self-regulating economy. Instead we have a new set of rules and procedures that is difficult to understand – even for experts and parliamentarians, let alone for ordinary citizens.

The unpalatable truth, admitted behind the scenes even by experts at the centre of the system, is that Europe's united money has not alleviated the European crisis: it has in fact been one of its principal causes. A series of seemingly stabilising economic developments has brought destabilisation beyond measure. Permanently fixed exchange rates and stable interest rates appeared to give greater security, but the very absence of financial market fluctuations snuffed out the possibility for adverse capital flows to impose corrective pressure for errant governments to change policies. Herman Van Rompuy, the scholarly former Belgian prime minister who, in 2010, became president of the EU's governing body, the European Council, has admitted that the euro's relatively problem-free start 'was like some kind of sleeping pill, some kind of drug'.[14]

Another broadside against the euro's governance failures, aimed particularly at the Eurogroup of European finance ministers, was launched by Mario Draghi. In May 2013, Draghi accused 'all the actors' in monetary union of suffering from 'long, complacent amnesia'; they had ignored for years the risks that were building up.[15] He accurately portrayed the division of Europe, separating 'countries with positive trade balances and sound budgets from those with growing budget deficits and external deficits … No one ever imagined that the monetary union could become a union divided between permanent creditors and permanent debtors, where the former would perpetually lend money and credibility to the latter.' In fact, as Draghi and others later realised, countries that transgressed against economic laws by living beyond their means were building up invisible penalties that they – and others – would discharge only later. The trail of unpaid debts and festering grievances would extend far into the future.

Five mutually reinforcing miscalculations contributed to the slow-burn build-up. First, the ECB's one-sided focus on achieving its 2 per cent inflation target diverted attention from problems in other fields, such as the stability of European banks. The ECB cannot be blamed for undue concentration on combating price rises, for its stance reflected political realities in Europe, particularly Germany's insistence that the new monetary system had to be built on Bundesbank-style anti-inflation rigour. However, excessive emphasis on fighting inflation – at a time when realising this goal was made significantly easier by globalisation-induced downward world-wide pressure on manufactured goods prices – encouraged complacency and hampered analysis of other policy areas where failures were looming. Ability to commit home-made mistakes was not a field, however, where the Europeans had a monopoly. Pre-financial crisis blunders by monetary authorities in the US and Britain were equally egregious.

Second, the belief that the 'one size fits all' monetary policy would lead to a symmetrical distribution of pain and gain was illusory. It was expected that faster-growing countries with above-average inflation and low interest rates at the beginning of monetary union would gain transitory benefits, but would suffer negative effects later, through reduced competitiveness that could no longer be rectified by devaluation. At the same time, low-inflation, low-growth countries such as Germany, which were held back at the beginning of the 2000s by interest rates that were too high for their own economic situation, would recover later, and this would help the rest of Europe. But these trends were not self-compensating. Germany used the earlier years of subdued growth to strengthen fundamentally its economic structures and has since been reaping the gains. Other countries enjoyed low interest rates and short-lived expansion without addressing structural reforms – and they have subsequently paid the price. Overall, the costs have exceeded the rewards, and over the lifetime of the euro the single currency has brought Europe a net deflationary bias.

The third error relates to the distortions in competitiveness that inevitably occur in a fixed exchange rate system that unites countries with different developments in prices and productivity. The idea was that these distortions could be reversed relatively easily, using a self-regulating process. Unfortunately, this has proved not to be the case. The early years of the euro opened up a competitiveness gap of around 30 per cent between Germany and southern European countries. This then started to close as the credit crisis and associated banking weaknesses ended the ability of the peripheral countries to borrow their way out of trouble. The competitiveness distortions are being reversed less rapidly than required because Germany (like other creditor countries, such as the Netherlands) is unwilling to undergo a period of radical reflation and weakening competitiveness in order to balance the debtor states' weakness. Those looking for economic stimulus and significantly higher inflation in Germany to rescue Europe's stragglers will end up disappointed.

Fourth, Europe had to retreat from the misplaced belief that low-cost financing could be arranged in perpetuity for countries with extreme current account surpluses and deficits. Politicians and technocrats knew the euro would be immune to currency crises. But they overlooked the fact that the system could be prone to credit crises, as lenders demanded higher interest rates on debt that was perceived to be of increasingly higher risk – even (or especially) after years of apparent convergence on the bond markets. The refusal of private sector creditors to provide more cash for the hard-up peripheral states brought in official lenders and harsh adjustment programmes that forcibly reduced the peripheral states' payments deficits, but allowed the creditor states to carry on generating large-scale surpluses. The burden of adjustment has been excessively skewed towards the deficit countries.

Fifth, finance ministers and central banks geared policies to limiting public debt and budget deficits – and neglected growth in private sector debt, which proved to be the euro bloc's Achilles' heel. Through the so-called Stability and Growth Pact agreed in 1997, euro members brought in rules for public debt monitoring. These were subsequently overridden by Germany and France during their phases of economic weakness in 2003–05, then suspended during the financial crisis, only to be reintroduced afterwards in modified form. However, by itself public debt provided an insufficient guide to the dangerous imbalances opening up: Ireland and Spain both registered budgetary surpluses in the years before their respective economic crashes. The formal rules of monetary union prevented policy-makers from looking at the explosive accumulation of private sector debt, with disastrous consequences. The litany of errors has left Europe riddled with rifts that provide built-in barriers to progress.

7 The technocrats stumble

THE EU bureaucracy – technocrats, officials, cadres from different backgrounds – faces the giant task of escaping the failures of the past in order to bring the euro crisis to a necessary resolution. In many cases, those responsible for past mistakes are still sitting at the levers of power. Government office has proved a fleeting experience for many forgettable euro political leaders, who have been swept into power on a wave of euphoria, only to be ejected in reaction to economic disappointment when the voters' mood turns nasty. The technical experts embedded into the euro mechanisms are the only ones with sufficient understanding and experience to keep the machine running. For many reasons, they are deeply reluctant to relinquish the instruments of control. Unfortunately, they are often the ones who, well beyond the daily headlines, have failed most abjectly. To investigate fully the origins of the euro crisis, a thoroughgoing analysis is needed of the role of the technocrats and of their interactions with politicians – a kind of Truth and Reconciliation Commission. That seems unlikely while the effects of uncertainty linger on. In the meantime, neither constructive progress nor an orderly retreat seems possible.

The gulf between initial perception and eventual reality is underlined by veteran Dutch central banker André Szász: 'Not one of the politicians who agreed the Maastricht treaty understood what they were doing.'[16] Confronted with the plethora of challenges, Europe's political class has been overwhelmed. Could the experts working for them have demonstrated better understanding, insight and execution skills? Unfortunately, the batteries of commissioners, directors and heads of mission in charge of the technical dossiers have generally revealed little more competence than their masters.

A fundamental failure of the euro's first decade was lack of awareness of the potential risk of rising balance of payments disequilibrium among member states. The European Central Bank, like other euro bloc institutions, neglected the danger that the capital markets and banks might one day choose no longer to finance growing current account deficits. Assuming that deficits and surpluses would be self-financing, the ECB published statistics for the euro bloc's combined balance of payments, but not for individual members. As long as the overall external picture was relatively balanced (which it was), everything appeared in order; the underlying components of a growing mechanism for vast financial disturbance did not seem to matter. Without giving any sign of noticing it, Europe's finest monetary experts were sitting on a powder keg.

In August 2007, as the US financial upheaval was starting to spill over to Europe, the ECB published a twelve-page analysis on the risks to global stability of world-wide payments imbalances in economies such as the US, China, Japan, Saudi Arabia and Russia. The experts highlighted the worrying US current account deficit (6.5 per cent of gross domestic product), but made no mention of the euro countries' much larger surpluses (Germany and the Netherlands) and deficits (Greece, Portugal and Spain). Otmar Issing, the ECB's chief economist for the first eight years of its existence, pointed out that monetary union greatly facilitated financing of current account balances. Writing before the sharp post-2010 rise in interest rate spreads between peripheral economy bonds and German government paper, he did however warn that the lack of 'risk premium on interest rates ... means that an important warning signal of undesirable developments with adverse repercussions is lost or becomes harder to discern'.[17]

The prime purveyor of unbridled optimism was the European Commission. In May 2008, just before the ECB's tenth anniversary, the Commission published a 328-page brochure gushing with exaggerated praise. Just two pages pointed to the problem of growing internal imbalances.[18] On its website, the Commission published a series of reassuring 'facts' about monetary union and denounced as 'myth' the assertion that 'some euro area member states suffer from economic problems in others'.[19] The truth was far more positive, the Commission affirmed: 'Governments coordinate their economic policies to ensure that all economies work harmoniously together ... The single currency itself also acts as a protective shield against external shocks ... Existing coordinating mechanisms mean that decisions can be taken quickly and smoothly – both in economic good times, and in the event of economic and financial difficulties.'[20]

All major European actors – the Eurogroup of finance

ministers, the ECB and the Commission – must share responsibility for the much-delayed recognition of problems building up behind the scenes. This catalogue of failure was bitterly attacked in 2012 by Jacques Delors, one of the euro's chief architects:

> If the finance ministers had wanted to get a clearer picture of the situation, they could have seen Ireland's extravagant behaviour with its banks, Spain's equally extravagant behaviour with mortgage lending, Greece's dissimulation of its real statistics. But they turned a blind eye. That is why I have always considered, since the beginning of the crisis, that the Eurogroup was morally and politically responsible for the crisis and that it should have reacted as early as 2008 to rectify its mistakes.[21]

Delors was adamant that the technocrats of the European Central Bank should accept their share of the blame:

> Spain, Greece, Ireland, Portugal and others thought they could make mistakes, protected by the euro. The trade balance between countries was disregarded. Nobody was concerned about that … At what moment did the governor of the [Central] Bank of Ireland, the governor of the Bank of Spain or other governors tell the ECB governing council that something was wrong? They did not say anything, nobody said a word. Therefore, they too are responsible for this situation. So, this is no time for them to lecture others.

At the centre of the euro system, Jean-Claude Trichet found it hard to distinguish between his conflicting roles as the single currency's promoter and as its policeman. Just before the financial crisis broke, in a series of speeches, lectures, press conferences and interviews, Trichet eulogised the advantages of monetary union, systematically glossed over errors of concept and implementation – and failed to see the dark clouds hovering overhead. Trichet repeatedly praised what was, in fact, the gravest signal of growing unreality – the convergence of Greek and German government bond prices, which he continually extolled as a sign of successful integration.[22]

In 2012, the ECB revised its view of events, and the Trichet doctrine was quietly buried. This amounted to tacit recognition that one-size-fits-all interest rates were one of the main causes of a string of calamitous euro upsets across the peripheral countries, most notably the effective bankruptcy of the Greek state in early 2012, in what was by far the world's biggest ever sovereign debt restructuring. Peter Praet, the bank's Belgian chief economist, drily observed that the earlier convergence of capital market interest rates around a German-based norm had caused 'moral hazard' by encouraging both creditors and debtors to take undue risks, for which they ultimately paid a high price.[23] Less than a year later, Vítor Constâncio, the former Portuguese finance minister and central bank chief who became deputy president of the ECB in 2010, went still further in revising the ECB's view of history. The euro's difficulties fell squarely in the area of money and credit, rather than public finance, said Constâncio. As the main problem, he identified private – not public – sector imbalances, 'financed by the banking sectors of the lending and borrowing countries'.[24] 'The inflow of relatively cheap financing turned into a huge credit boom in the countries now under stress.' The credit boom in the then fast-growing peripheral countries was not, at the time, a matter of concern for the ECB. Undoubtedly, the technocrats have learned lessons from their errors. Some of those to blame may even, over time, admit where they went wrong. The fading of the scars left by the experience may take longer.

8 A bank unlike the others

On a sunny morning in late July 2012, in the chandeliered splendour of Lancaster House in London's West End, an important milestone was set in the short history of the euro. The stately mansion, built almost two centuries ago for Britain's Hanoverian royal family, was once the glittering venue for society balls. Today the building is used for official seminars and receptions when the British establishment wants to make a good impression, particularly on influential foreigners. On the eve of the opening of the Olympic Games, this was the venue for a promotional government conference as a showpiece for UK manufacturing and services. Mario Draghi, president of the European Central Bank, was one of the guests of honour. Draghi came not to support British business, but to shore up the euro. He succeeded. But the steps he outlined left question marks over the amorphous nature of his multinational bank – a central bank unlike the others, whose lack of clear contours is a principal reason for lingering euro uncertainties.

Draghi opened his short address with quixotic humour, comparing the euro to a bumblebee: 'This is a mystery of nature because it shouldn't fly but instead it does.'[25] Nevertheless he had a serious message. At the height of international capital market gloom about the single currency, speculators had been selling the euro and dumping the bonds of countries like Italy and Spain. The central bank president thought anti-euro action had gone too far – and he said so: 'Within our mandate, the ECB is ready to do whatever it takes to preserve the euro. And believe me, it will be enough.' His words reverberated around the world, propelling sharply higher bond prices for the countries that had previously been attacked and procuring important breathing space for the single currency. But what was effectively a masterly bluff to counter the pessimists and keep crisis countries' bond yield just below what he later termed 'panic levels' laid bare important weaknesses in the euro's defensive machinery.[26] Many market participants assumed that Draghi's announcement signalled agreement with the German central bank, the Bundesbank, to underpin the weaker euro countries through joint bond-buying action. In fact, as the following days and weeks were to show, this was not the case.

In the immediate aftermath of the London statement, Draghi's largely unprepared ECB colleagues worked hard to assemble a strategic blueprint to lend detail to the spare contours of the announcement. They constructed a programme for the central bank to intervene to buy the bond issues of struggling countries, provided they met stringent agreements on economic belt-tightening with the European Commission and the International Monetary Fund. But Draghi's big idea, although it continued to have a positive psychological effect on the financial markets, remained ambiguous. It had a resounding deterrent impact, even though there were doubts as to whether it would ever be put into practice.

The reasons for this contradiction lie in the ECB's peculiar structure. In contrast to the Federal Reserve, the Bank of Japan or the Bank of England, the ECB cannot intervene at will to stabilise conditions in any specific country or economic area. This was, in addition, a significant impediment to the effectiveness of the across-the-board (for all euro member states except Greece) 'quantitative easing' bond purchases started by the ECB in March 2015. The ECB was unable specifically to target the southern member states that were suffering most from a fragmentation of credit conditions throughout the euro bloc, an important factor adding further to economic pressures, lowering growth and employment in a broad swathe of countries around the Mediterranean. Despite some progress towards becoming a 'normal' central bank, the institution is the prime symbol of the unfinished state of monetary union – a single monetary body facing not just one political counterweight, but nineteen different nations with more or less sovereign powers.

The ultimate stability of a currency lies not in the technical ability of the central bank to print money, but in the resilience of the economy and the political and fiscal authorities behind it. The euro remains a currency in search of a state, the centrepiece of an imbalanced and frequently incompatible series of relationships between different countries' central banking and governmental responsibilities. The ECB's uneven nature weakens monetary union by raising uncertainty over its ability to resist economic attrition, greatly complicating the task of crisis management.

In line with its penchant for coining impenetrable acronyms, the ECB termed the technical instrument that was eventually formed in the wake of Draghi's London remarks the OMT programme, standing for Outright Monetary Transactions. In fact, as soon became evident, the new tool was neither monetary nor outright – nor did it lead to any transactions. The essence of the OMT was its conditionality, since bond purchases by the central bank – highly controversial in Germany because they were viewed as potentially inflationary – could be brought into play only by governments that signed up to strict austerity packages with the European Union and the IMF. And no country around Europe was ready to make new commitments on this. In particular, the widespread vote in the February 2013 Italian elections against the economic restructuring of the government led by Mario Monti made it highly unlikely that the new government in Rome would use the facility. The same was true, for similar reasons, of the hard-pressed administration in Madrid. As the campaign for Germany's elections in September 2013 got under way, German scepticism about the OMT hardened, opening holes in Draghi's safety net that made it effectively inoperable.

The doubts increased when the German press published a twenty-nine-page Bundesbank document setting out its evidence to the German constitutional court that any OMT bond purchases would be illegal. The court was still months away from passing judgement, yet the ECB could hardly go ahead with the programme when the highest court in the largest economy and the biggest creditor had not decided on its validity. On financial markets, however, the truce held. A rally continued in the bond markets of countries like Spain, Italy,

Ireland and Portugal, mainly a result of a wave of international liquidity entering Europe in search of higher interest rates, driven by substantial credit-easing measures in the US and Japan. But the ceasefire was fragile. Central bankers everywhere maintained an outpouring of cautionary statements about exaggerated exuberance on the financial markets. Ominously, European economies remained in recession. In a sense, Draghi's proclamation was counterproductive, since it gave the impression that the central bank was coming to the rescue of monetary union. This reduced the pressure on governments in the problem-plagued countries to take urgent remedial action of their own through much-needed but unpopular structural reforms. Draghi's statement was also welcome news to Angela Merkel, for the ECB's move took the pressure off the German government to decide its own kind of direct fiscal backstop for hard-up southern states – a measure that Merkel would have found difficult if not impossible to push through parliament.

This was a near-insoluble dilemma for the central bank, poised between the two extreme perceptions of not doing enough 'to save the euro' – or doing too much, as the permanent drumbeat of German opposition to Draghi's salvage plan underlined. As time went on after the Lancaster House speech, and as the ECB moved towards outright quantitative easing in March 2015, it became increasingly obvious that Draghi's plan for reviving Europe was greatly dependent on forcing down the value of the euro to give a fillip to European exports. An extraordinary statement by the ECB chief in August 2014 praising 'the fundamentals for a weaker exchange rate', and revealing (highly unusually for a central banker) that 'other central banks have been reducing their exposure to the euro', provided a strong indication of the ECB's fundamental stance – a clear contradiction of traditional German policies since the 1960s favouring a strong currency.[27] Europe's lack of consensus on the way out of the debt crisis gave the ECB little choice but to advance to the front line; yet at the same time it confronted the ECB with the risk of overexposure, opposition and setbacks. This led to inevitable disappointment that, for all the pride and potency invested in the euro project, the ECB would not, and indeed could not, be equal to the task.

9 The Cyprus cauldron

EASTER-TIME in the eastern Mediterranean can be chilly. But in March 2013 nobody in Cyprus expected the banks to freeze up. This divided island, split between Greece and Turkey after the Turkish invasion of 1974, yet a member of the European Union since 2004 and of monetary union since 2008, is an appropriately complicated place for the euro's myriad contradictions to burst to the surface. Under the financial rescue for the island that was decided by European governments in March 2013, larger depositors in leading Cypriot banks were reduced to the status of unsecured creditors and had to accept heavy losses as part of an overall bailout package. The upheaval in the euro bloc's second-smallest member (after Malta) set a harrowing precedent for other countries. The Cyprus affair amply illustrates the inchoate state of decision-making when nations share a common money, yet remain politically independent – any remedial action that genuinely resolves underlying problems is virtually impossible.

The Cyprus deal followed earlier financial rescues for Greece, Ireland, Portugal and Spain. It was one more example of Europe salvaging a country crippled by policy mistakes that were made worse by euro membership. In this case, joining the euro bloc drove Cyprus's banks and a vast array of ancillary businesses – lawyers, accountants, financial consultants and associated hangers-on – to double the size of the financial sector between 2006 and 2011. The island attracted deposits from such troubled countries as Russia, Lebanon and former Yugoslavia, and it poured money into risky ventures abroad – including in the even more financially stricken country of Greece. The build-up of the Cypriot financial bubble underlined yet again the perversion of the euro's grand aims. And the solution set off another procession of unintended consequences – problems that blocked progress towards more European solidarity, especially in Germany. Somewhat ominously, Chancellor Angela Merkel's domestic popularity increased as a result of what was widely seen as tough German action against the southern miscreants.

Cyprus is a story of shoddy governance, extravagant dreams and abrupt betrayal. A microstate accounting for the ludicrously low proportion of 0.2 per cent of the euro bloc's economic output was catapulted into the headlines by revelations of a double life as a cauldron of financial malpractice and diplomatic intrigue. In 1989, more than two years before the Maastricht treaty, Bundesbank President Karl Otto Pöhl presciently forecast 'considerable resistance' from the German people once they understood that monetary union 'centres on their money'.[28] As a result of the Cyprus agreement, legions of savers across Europe began to fear – rightly or wrongly – government expropriation of their money. Telling account holders that their savings could be raided to restore banking solvency had a sobering psychological effect, especially on the German population. They possess the largest savings in bank accounts in Europe, and they now believe that they could eventually be compelled to stump up for the folly of bankers and the miscalculations of bureaucrats. At the height of the Cypriot imbroglio, the Bundesbank stoked the fire by publishing European data showing that average German household wealth was much lower than in Spain, Italy and Cyprus.[29] The unspoken message was that unreliable southerners had been enriching themselves at Germany's expense.

In other ways, too, the Cyprus agreement had deleterious effects. It reimposed the link between the finances of the country's overextended banks – which had used the formerly benign conditions of monetary union to overstretch disastrously their deposit-taking and lending businesses – and those of the government. The European Union had already seen how countries with previously sound finances (such as Ireland) could suffer jolting setbacks through the need to support shaky banks. Europe brought in policies in summer 2012 to break the vicious circle under which governments piled up more debt to rescue impecunious banks, causing higher interest costs, which then increased the banks' problems and led to still more public debt. But in spring 2013, as European creditor countries' patience finally snapped and money for bailouts started to run out, the fate of the hard-hit Cyprus government, of the island's hopelessly overexposed banks, and of the euro bloc as a whole were revealed as inextricably intertwined.

The public relations blow was worsened by European finance ministers' support for the Cyprus government's original plan to impose a tax on smaller savers in Cypriot banks with accounts of less than €100,000. This was later rescinded, under a hail of protest that extended well beyond Cyprus, in favour of larger write-downs exclusively on the larger depositors, many of them from Russia. The punitive levy, coupled with the closure of Laiki Bank, the island's second-biggest bank, affected many foreign account holders dabbling in money-laundering and other dubious practices, as well as businesses, institutions and individuals with legitimate deposits. And it raised the question of how the island could pay back its huge remaining debt if its economic mainstay – financial services – was to be severely curtailed.

Amid open talk of Cyprus quitting the single currency, and with Britain's Royal Air Force sending in a plane with emergency supplies of euro banknotes for military personnel on the island, Cyprus broke another euro taboo by imposing capital controls, outlawed under European law for anything except to protect 'public safety' in a national emergency. A heated dispute between the European Union and the Moscow government over the treatment of Russian depositors added to the foreign policy ramifications. Russian Prime Minister Dmitry Medvedev accused Cyprus of 'stealing' from big deposit holders. Cypriot Archbishop Chrysostomos II, representing the Greek Orthodox Church, which said it was placing its considerable wealth at the country's disposal at its hour of need, said of the single currency: 'With the brains that they have in Brussels, it is certain that it will not last in the long term, and the best is to think about how to escape it.'

The Cypriot rescue was a Byzantine plot of bewildering complexity. All the presidents of the various European institutions – the ECB, the Commission, the Council, the Eurogroup of finance ministers – plus the head of the IMF assembled in Brussels for hours of frenzied parleying with Cypriot President Nicos Anastasiades, whose family conveniently wired €21 million from Laiki Bank to London in the days before the rescue talks started. The affair underlined the tortuous process of getting anything done in Europe. In China, as a Chinese business stalwart pointed out shortly afterwards, a recalcitrant governor of a province of Cyprus's size would have been summoned to the state council and given ten minutes to redeem himself, or else be fired.

At the end of the negotiations, Jeroen Dijsselbloem, the Dutch head of the Eurogroup of finance minsters, heaped on the pain by terming the Cypriot raid on deposits a possible template for future European bank salvage work. In tones of no-nonsense Calvinism, Dijsselbloem declared that European banks had to shrink to manageable size: 'Strengthen your banks, fix your balance sheets and realise that if a bank gets in trouble, the response will no longer automatically be that we'll come and take away your problem.'[30] Under the Dijsselbloem doctrine, the northern creditors will no longer dispense favours to debtors in the south. Cypriot capital controls cleaved through the indivisibility of the single currency. A euro effectively no longer had the same value across the regions of monetary union. In previous years, taxpayers in better-off countries bore the brunt of bailout packages. In Cyprus, this practice stopped. On a sunny island that suddenly turned shady, monetary theories clashed with geopolitical realities – and the creditors' will prevailed. The message reverberated throughout Europe: all parts of the euro bloc are equal, but some are more equal than others. It is a lesson that, two years later, would hold particular relevance for the classic focus of euro neuralgia: Greece.

10 Greek tussles, euro sovereignty

YANIS VAROUFAKIS, who took over as Greek finance minister in January 2015 and held the post for five action-packed months, was an unlikely officeholder from an impossible country. Varoufakis, economic standard-bearer of the far-left Syriza government which came to power as the result of widespread voter hostility to the austerity measures decreed by Greece's creditors, did whatever it took during his short tenure in office to stoke the hostility of his finance minister peers in the Eurogroup.

A motorbike-straddling university lecturer with a self-confident fondness for outrageous soundbites, Varoufakis achieved much publicity but had little direct success with his brand of hectoring rhetoric against the iniquity of the creditors' medicine. He won no prizes for diplomacy, telling fellow European governments and the media that Greece was bankrupt, terming Italian debt unsustainable, and summoning up war claims on Germany which decades ago were deemed unpayable. Varoufakis's strength lay in his and the system's weakness. His trump card was the contagion of Greek uncertainty and instability. Because of the near-universal fear that, if Greece were to leave the euro, the resulting turbulence (political and economic) would be much worse than if it remained inside, Varoufakis and Alexis Tsipras, the Syriza leader and Greek prime minister, maintained Greece within the single currency, with the perspective of winning major debt restructuring from its creditors, led by Germany.

Greece's ability to turn its own very poor negotiating position into a form of victory underlined a strange paradox about the management of the euro. Individual states have relinquished sovereignty over their currencies, but instead of pooling it (as was intended) in a cohesive and constructive way to improve the functioning of the system as a whole, they have tended to exploit the interdependence of the euro area as a means of doing harm to each other.

One acute observer of the single currency's functioning is Athanasios Orphanides, a former Federal Reserve economist who was governor of the Bank of Cyprus, the central bank, for five years after the island state joined the euro in 2007. Commenting on what he called the 'original sin' of the onerous rescue plan for Greece decided by its European creditors in May 2010, Orphanides stated in summer 2015:

Five years after the original sin, the collapse of Greece is continuing. The crisis in Greece is a symptom of a wider problem. Member states that joined the euro area relinquished national crisis management tools. This makes euro area member states perceived as weak exceptionally vulnerable to exploitation by member states perceived as strong. The ease with which the euro was exploited to shift crisis-related costs from one member state to another in May 2010 created a precedent that dominated throughout the euro area crisis. The precedent invited exploitation of the weak by the strong, violating fundamental principles and European ideals and creating resentment and mistrust among the people of Europe ... No effort has been made to stop governments in one state from inflicting harm on other states ... The current framework has encouraged conflict over cooperation. This has proven disastrous for the euro area as a whole and ultimately for Europe.[31]

The melancholy truth is that genuine abandonment of sovereignty – rather than simply pooling it, as countries do routinely in areas where they maintain some semblance of control in international groupings – would be necessary in three areas to secure smooth running in the monetary bloc. First, countries would have to submit to thoroughgoing European control of their economic and budgetary systems, in order to ensure that they do not place unnecessary operating risks on the other members of the euro bloc. Second, they would need to pledge taxpayers' funds for cross-border rescues of other countries (or their banking networks) that get into trouble. Third, they would have to give up a much greater share of tax revenues than hitherto, and indeed to give central European institutions the capability to raise their own tax revenue, to channel extra funds throughout the monetary bloc and to iron out structural disparities. This adds up to a cocktail of requirements to which no euro member appears ready to agree.

Euro states have been spurred by post-2010 setbacks to

decide on a series of steps to strengthen the bloc's internal arrangements. The European Commission has been given the opportunity to influence the budgets of the nineteen euro-area countries on a previously unimaginable scale, through a strengthening of the Stability and Growth Pact, but there are strong doubts whether it will be able to wield these powers to good effect if confronted by resistance from determined member states. Member states have set up a permanent rescue fund – the €500 billion European Stability Mechanism – to buttress states in need, and this has helped calm concerns about the financing requirements of the hardest-hit members. Because the EU is unable to meet the financing needed to hold the monetary union together from its own budget, harnessing taxpayers' funds from creditor countries to keep the euro afloat will sustain lively debate in coming years. Germany, ever more suspicious of plans for mutualisation of debts, is likely to approve funds only for the more stable, better-off euro countries with a higher credit rating – countries that do not require extra support.

From the beginning, sovereignty has been a key stumbling block in European deliberations on a common money. As long ago as 1964, the Bundesbank said that nascent plans for monetary union formulated by the European Commission would have to be accompanied by a political union with 'transfer of national sovereignty' – a position it doggedly repeated in coming decades. In the years before the introduction of the euro, Germany's rising financial influence increased its neighbours' desire for a new form of economic organisation that would allow them to regain monetary powers effectively ceded to Germany. The Bundesbank's might grew to such an extent that the Banque de France complained in the 1970s about the 'tyranny of the D-Mark', while Parisian government officials carped about Germany's 'currency hegemony'. President Mitterrand called the D-Mark 'Germany's nuclear weapon'. Felipé Gonzalez, Spanish prime minister during the 1980s and a key Mitterrand ally, viewed formal transfers of powers to a new European Central Bank as a means of getting back leverage that had long since disappeared: 'We give up sovereignty to regain sovereignty.' There was always concern, though, that countries would see only the positive side of this message, and ignore the negative part. As always, the Bundesbank pointed an admonitory finger. Hans Tietmeyer, the German central bank president in the period immediately before the introduction of the euro, continually emphasised that monetary union would bring great constraints: 'Monetary union means restricting national sovereignty, national freedom of action and unilateralism. In a monetary union, countries need to address and solve their economic problems and challenges in a similar manner and at a similar pace.'

Such caveats were largely ignored, but they proved prescient. The old dream of a functioning supranational order, in which member countries would pool their individual strengths to reinforce their joint capacity to act, has not worked. Countries have ceded powers under the force of negative events; but the rewards have proved elusive. Governments in Greece, Ireland, Portugal, Spain and Cyprus have been compelled by the intervention of the European Union and the IMF to give up national independence in many aspects of economic policy. But since internal exchange rates in the euro bloc have been abolished, the IMF does not have the power to drive through one measure it normally prescribes in cases of grave economic imbalance: formal currency devaluation. As a consequence, severe restructuring measures are all the more painful for the countries' populations, producing social and political upheaval.

This harsh atmosphere is hardly conducive to euro bloc members agreeing further funding for mutual support or to a pooling of European government debt through so-called 'eurobonds', under which member states would share liability for common debt issuance – a step that Germany has ruled out as contravening the no-bailout clause of the Maastricht treaty. Once again, the Berlin government is caught in the crossfire of attacks from different sides. Euro supporters charge that Germany's intransigent lack of generosity is destabilising the currency system, whereas sceptics say the Germans have already done quite enough. They are maintaining a flow of legal action in the German constitutional court to try to impede any further funding. In September 2012, the court gave the green light to a new permanent rescue fund, the European Stability Mechanism, on condition that Germany's liability should not exceed €190 billion. The other important issue – whether the European Central Bank was legally permitted to intervene and buy hard-pressed countries' state bonds in a selective manner – has been left undecided after a string of complex legal judgments.

Beyond the technical and constitutional worries about the validity and usefulness of the rescue schemes, concern has grown about whether they are democratically legitimate. Many people across Europe, in both creditor and debtor countries, are concerned at the euro's transformation into an oversized artificial life-support machine, far removed from a self-regulating economic order. This transfer of control to shadowy financial mechanisms run by technocrats is a long way from the more benign abdication of sovereignty in the interests of solidarity and joint well-being foreseen by the fathers of Maastricht. It also contrasts with the principles of democratic legitimacy that imbued the development of the European Community in the 1950s and 1960s – and indeed that inspired countries in the old Soviet empire to break free from the shackles of communism and join a democratic Europe following the upheavals of the late 1980s. These multiple worries have further hampered euro members' desire to proceed further down the path of genuine power-sharing, reducing the chances of progress towards a genuine fiscal union.

In the absence of a real fiscal partnership, under which national parliaments give up sway over tax and spending decisions, the rules limiting government budget deficits, under the modified Stability and Growth Pact, are unlikely to provide a sustainable route to standardised fiscal behaviour. Electorates who believe they are the most likely to have to pay for others' mistakes are the keenest to restore the sanctity of the no-bailout clause that prevents states from standing behind the debts of others. The German view is that the financial markets acquiesced in the exaggerated under-pricing of debt risks in the initial years of monetary union because 'moral hazard' prevailed: many market participants believed the no-bailout clause was in abeyance, opening the way for the peripheral countries' boom-to-bust helter-skelter. According to this interpretation, the way to redemption lies not in transfers of sovereignty, but in every country standing on its own two feet. Even though in some ways it undercuts the basic credo behind the single currency, this concept may come back into vogue in coming years, as the euro bloc digests the lessons of past turbulence.

11 Fear holds the key

Opposing fears about the outcome of monetary union act as a decisive block on sensible decision-making. One reason why the German political establishment – both left and right – has so far lined up in favour of bailouts of weaker euro countries, led by Greece, is the widespread concern in Germany that a break-up of the monetary bloc would lead to a new German currency that would sharply appreciate compared with the present euro. This, it is feared, would bring a catastrophic collapse of German trade with the rest of Europe, with disastrous consequences for the entire European Union. Others, on the opposing wing of the debate, are fiercely critical of such support measures, which they see as open-ended subsidies for mismanaged euro member states – subsidies that could pave the way for calamitous debauchment of the currency, with ensuing social and economic unrest.

Particularly in Germany, dissenters from the perennial policy of 'more Europe' are routinely castigated for their lack of political correctness. Instead of constructive dialogue between the two sides of the argument, we see a continued tendency for decision-making paralysis, generated not by rational debate but by terror about the outcome of alternative policies. Such an environment provides fertile ground for political gerrymandering, distortions and blackmail of all kinds.

Although political parties opposed to the single currency have become more important in the electorate arithmetic of nearly all member states, so far the pro- and anti-euro sides of the argument have simply cancelled each other out – an uneasy stalemate that will probably continue. There has been no wholesale clear-out of the old guard. Although – with the prime exceptions of Angela Merkel in Germany and Mark Rutte in the Netherlands – government leaders in euro members have been ejected in the wake of popular discontent over austerity and recession, Europe has seen inflections rather than sweeping political changes: variants of the political parties that led countries into the euro and that presided over the ill-starred combination of boom and bust are still in power nearly everywhere. A novelty has been the arrival on the scene of a serious-minded, relatively well-organised anti-euro party in Germany in the form of Alternative for Germany, which has hardened the overall nature of German political discourse on the single currency.

Fear seldom provides an appropriate foundation for sensible decision-making; yet it has been a constant companion to monetary union – from the basic reasons for its establishment, all the way through to the choice of participants. The French, well aware of German recalcitrance over giving up the D-Mark, were nearly always able to operate the levers of bilateral diplomacy to fulfil their purposes – but with dexterity and effectiveness that declined over time. One of the masterminds behind the euro,

European Commission President Jacques Delors, more than once orchestrated a political crisis to force the Germans to move forward. Edouard Balladur, France's former conservative finance minister, promoted a French 'Yes' to the country's referendum on the Maastricht treaty in September 1992 as a tool to control Germany. Balladur, who later became prime minister, was a mentor of both ECB President Jean-Claude Trichet and French President Nicolas Sarkozy. His rationale was a thinly veiled plea to those who feared the reunited nation would be all-powerful: '[French] rejection of the treaty will not give France any more liberty; it will simply allow Germany to act as it desires, without taking heed of its neighbours or its partners, without being constrained by any set of common European rules in its role as a military, economic, financial and monetary power in the centre of the continent.'[32] The French electorate approved Maastricht by a tiny margin, with trepidation about different outcomes playing a big role on both sides of the debate. An opinion poll showed that 21 per cent of French 'Yes' voters wished to counter German dominance of Europe, while a still larger proportion of 'No' voters (40 per cent) took a diametrically opposite view, turning down the treaty on the grounds that it would increase German power.

German support in the late 1990s for including Italy as a founding member of the euro, despite well-publicised doubts about its economic resilience, was partly motivated by concern that, if left outside the single currency, Italy would devalue the lira and play havoc with German industrial trade. Otmar Issing, a member of the Bundesbank board and later the ECB's chief economist, was well known as a hawk on monetary union. But he said the currency crises of 1992–93, when the lira was devalued by 30 per cent, bankrupting many competing southern German firms, represented a defining moment: 'I and others came to the conclusion that the common market would not survive another such currency crisis.'[33]

Opposing horror scenarios are close to the surface of all decision-making on the euro's future. The Greek electorate was regularly told it would 'commit suicide' if it voted against austerity measures. Investors such as George Soros, who famously made $1 billion by speculating against sterling in 1992, emphasise how monetary union pits creditors' fears of losing money against debtors' equal and opposite anxieties about being locked into a permanent cycle of deepening debt and depression.[34] German industrialists regularly lay bare their susceptibility to blackmail by deficit-ridden debtor states by voicing their apprehension about the shattering impact of a rising currency. Hans-Peter Keitel, president of the German Industry Federation, warned in 2012 of the enormous danger of a euro break-up: 'Every step backwards in European integration would mean incalculable risks for the economic and political stability.' Non-German politicians take grim pleasure in pointing out that future currency adjustments could bring Germany to its knees. Laurent Fabius, a veteran of thirty years of on-off Franco-German monetary disputes, who became foreign minister in 2012 under socialist President François Hollande, hinted (as an opposition politician at the end of 2010) that, if its eastern neighbour decided to leave the euro, France would take an ultra-hard line in forcing up the German exchange rate. His prediction was that the new German currency would face a revaluation of 100 per cent, with a devastating impact on Germany's competitiveness.[35] Disquiet and unease on different sides maintain a precarious balance. Monetary union is kept going by fear of what would ensue if it ever came crashing to the ground.

12 Germany's limits

GERMANY CANNOT and will not stimulate its economy sufficiently to lead the distressed southern nations out of the economic abyss. Trade and investment relations between Germany and the euro periphery have been steadily reduced. So even if the Germans were willing to give in to their neighbours' insistence on Keynesian demand measures to promote their domestic economic recovery, this would have little positive effect. Germany's economic interests are growing increasingly in the direction of European countries outside monetary union, such as Poland, Russia and Turkey, as well as faster-growing new markets in countries like Brazil, China, Indonesia, India and South Africa.

The Germans are willing to make sacrifices for the good of Europe, but they have their limits. This became evident when I took part in a debate on the euro in May 2009 with an audience of around two hundred invited burghers in Hamburg. The duel on the motion 'Is the euro irreversible?' was with a seasoned member of the European parliament. I proclaimed the view that the European monetary union might not last, pointing to the widening inflation gap between north and south, the lack of political union, and the large-scale expansion of current account deficits. At the outset, on a show of hands, 161 members of the audience said they believed monetary union was irreversible, while only 48 thought it might not last. After a lively ninety-minute discussion, the numbers agreeing with me had increased to 82, while those in favour of the motion had fallen to 122. The margin believing the euro would last forever had shrunk by two-thirds, from 113 to only 40. What was the reason for the turnaround? Simple. I put the question: 'Who's going to pay for it all?' If rising economic imbalances were not corrected over time, I argued, large transfers would be needed from the better-performing countries to the worse-performing; the only way to guarantee monetary union was for the Germans to subsidise the others permanently. As with the wider German public, this was not a concept that the audience much cared for – as has become evident in the ensuing four years.

Over this period, the southern countries have made great exertions to correct previously overheated economies, by freezing growth, reducing incomes and significantly increasing unemployment. Higher demand for these countries' exports would be more necessary than ever to compensate for tightened belts at home. Unfortunately, the world environment has not been propitious – unlike the situation in Germany in 2003–05, during the ultimately successful reforms introduced by Chancellor Gerhard Schröder. Back then, credit-fuelled booms in those peripheral countries that subsequently got into trouble stoked demand for German exports – compensation for Germany's lower domestic growth caused by economic restructuring. Occasionally self-righteous recommendations by the Germans that southern countries simply need to imitate what Germany did a decade before have no great relevance; the two episodes a decade apart are simply not comparable.

In similar manner, Angela Merkel's frequent reminders that foreigners should not exaggerate Germany's capacity to resolve the debt crisis, and her warnings about overextending her country's strengths, are partly a tactical gesture to shift the Germans out of the firing line. But there is more to it than that. Regular demands from abroad that Germany should use its relatively favourable public debt and borrowing position to undertake large-scale reflation in order to resolve the European tangle are wide of the mark, for three reasons. First, many of these recommendations stem from Anglo-Saxon economists, who overlook important differences in behaviour: the Germans react to various kinds of stimulus measures very differently from the British and the Americans. Tax cuts in Germany very often lead Germans to save more – the opposite of what is intended – because of a peculiar form of German cynicism. Ordinary taxpayers fear that subsequent increases in budget deficits will be financed, sooner or later, by putting taxes up again. Attempts at economic stimulus through government-sponsored public works programmes often have the same effect in stimulating savings – even though there are valid grounds for higher infrastructure spending. A similar lack of positive response can be expected from attempts to boost demand in Germany through further European Central Bank interest rate cuts and government bond purchases under the quantitative easing programme belatedly started in March 2015, especially now that repeated credit easing has reduced interest rates to below zero. This was a highly unpopular sanction against the elderly savers who are an important segment of the German population and who represent a leading source of scepticism and opposition regarding the single currency.

Second, radical reflation could divert attention from the real economic problems of the peripheral countries, caused by the juxtaposition of the wrong internal European exchange rates and faulty choices in industrial and structural policies. Now that much-needed adjustment and consolidation are under way on the periphery, promoting relief through short-term demand stimulus in Germany and other stronger nations would probably do more harm than good. The main priority is for the problem countries to overcome the weaknesses in their economic structures, for example by building effective education and training systems in modern industrial sectors, such as advanced manufacturing, internet technology, telecommunications and software. These programmes take years to put into effect. However, over time, extension of proven German systems in industrial training and apprenticeships will bring greater benefits to crisis-hit euro members than subsidies for outdated industries or for unnecessary infrastructure.

Third, economic calculations show that efforts to boost wage growth in Germany, as demanded by many foreign experts, would only temporarily increase consumer demand. Because many German companies are exposed to intense globalised competition, artificially induced wage increases that go well beyond productivity improvements would end up reducing investment, output and jobs. Imports would rise, but because of the rise in Germany's trade with non-euro countries, and the relatively minor amount of commerce conducted with the hard-hit single currency members, the countries that need greatest relief would derive only small benefits.

Those pondering such considerations must bear in mind that a major reason why France, Italy and other European governments backed monetary union was a desire to weaken economically newly reunified Germany. Overloading demands on Germany to provide assistance to other euro members could indeed undermine Germany's overall economic resilience, with negative effects on the whole of Europe. One of the Berlin government's most valid arguments for resisting such demands lies in pointing out that overextending Germany's capabilities could deprive it (and possibly other creditor countries) of their prized triple-A credit rating. This would weaken the ability of the diverse European euro support mechanisms to raise funds on foreign markets for channelling to the hard-up euro states.

According to one theoretical solution to the single currency's travails, Berlin would authorise loosening of Europe-wide austerity policies, accept full-scale debt mutualisation through Europe-wide eurobonds, and take macroeconomic measures to boost inflation to 4 per cent and move into a current account deficit on the balance of payments. Such a package would, however, be politically unfeasible – and for good reason. Overstretching German capabilities would render not just Germany but the whole of Europe a disservice. Former Chancellor Willy Brandt correctly said that the biggest risk for European stability stemmed from a weak, not a strong Germany. Navigating the path between strength and weakness will strain European nerves for some time to come.

13 The French connection

FUNDAMENTAL DISAGREEMENTS over monetary union are increasing between the two key member states, Germany and France, amid much questioning over the compatibility of the two countries' objectives and methods. As has been made clear by conflicting statements from President François Hollande and Chancellor Angela Merkel, France wants 'solidarity' while Germany seeks 'competitiveness'. The duo accounts for roughly half the economic output of the nineteen-country bloc. Yet their structural ideas on renewing Europe appear far apart; communication between the two governments is at a low ebb; and mutual willingness to make concessions to help each other is fading.

None of this is completely new. Mirroring past patterns, most notably those of Hollande's predecessor, President Nicolas Sarkozy, adversity has drawn the French and German leaders together. The terrorist attacks on Paris in January and November 2015 drew Merkel to symbolically visit the French capital as well as to express support and solidarity. But below the surface, antagonism over the motivation and objectives of monetary union remains as important as ever. Notably, France will use mounting concern over Europe's external and internal security as justification for increased funding for law and order measures and border reinforcements – measures that will be exempt from European strictures restraining public spending. Key differences between Germany and France over the economic and political prerequisites for monetary union have dogged the European project for more than fifty years. The Franco-German relationship has been the pivot of post-war European recovery, but it now faces tensions that severely constrain Europe's ability to prosper in the years ahead. Merkel will not be looking forward to the possibility that Sarkozy, promulgating a far more nationalist agenda than when he was in power between 2007–12, will return to the Élysée Palace in spring 2017 (assuming he wins the nomination by the French conservative opposition party to fight against Hollande in the April–May 2017 presidential election). That would present Merkel with a highly uncomfortable four- or five-month interregnum with a populist French leader increasingly opposed to key tenets of European integration before the German parliamentary election scheduled for September or October 2017.

Germany's relations with France have been a story of fluctuating political tandems: from post-war leaders Konrad Adenauer and Charles de Gaulle, to Helmut Schmidt and Valéry Giscard d'Estaing in the 1970s and Helmut Kohl and François Mitterrand in the 1980s. In the past twenty years, the interaction has grown more fragile. With reunification and the relocation of the government from Bonn to Berlin, a new generation of German politicians and civil servants has come to the fore, less patient, more self-confident, and less likely to pay homage to the *Grande Nation*.

A precarious marriage of convenience between Gerhard Schröder and Jacques Chirac gave way to another inconsistent alliance linking Nicolas Sarkozy and Angela Merkel. In May 2012 came a new change of style as Hollande moved into the Elysée Palace, a bland replacement for Sarkozy's febrile hyperactivity. The new French leader is linked to his Berlin counterpart by bonds of mutual indifference: Hollande and Merkel have never tried to hide their lack of empathy. Merkel set a downward spiral in train a few months before the French elections in spring 2012 by despatching a senior official from her Christian Democrat Party to tell a pro-Sarkozy French party rally that Hollande represented 'outdated concepts and left-wing dreams from the ragbag of politics'. The new French president has spoken of 'friendly tensions' between the two countries, remarking that Merkel 'doesn't have the same ideas as I do'. The German chancellor's pursed-lipped description of the French connection is 'not uncomplicated'.

Even the resilient 1980s relationship between Kohl and Mitterrand was marked by swirling disagreements. Now more than ever, a curious symbiosis binds the two countries. France needs an outwardly robust Germany to camouflage the extent to which the French have fallen from grace in the economic and political stakes over the past twenty years. And for Germany, the appendage of an apparently confident (but in reality seriously weakened) France is a profoundly useful device to conceal from the rest of the world an inconvenient rise in German power.

For half a century, every stage of the epochal journey to monetary union has been marked by Franco-German contradictions and tensions. In a timeless remark from 1970, Otmar Emminger, one of the Bundesbank's main post-war figures (and later its president), commented: 'The French want to put shackles as quickly as possible on what they see as our sinister German monetary policy.'[36] Shortly after Mitterrand's election in May 1981, Emminger's successor, Karl Otto Pöhl, suggested that France should temporarily leave the European Monetary System, the precursor of monetary union.[37] In 1989, Mitterrand laid bare his antipathy to central banking independence, which he saw as a cover for German power: 'The [European] Monetary System is already a German zone. But the Federal Republic of Germany does not have authority over our economies. With the [European] Central Bank it would have it.'[38]

Plus ça change! Hollande, the man who served Mitterrand in the Elysée as a (very) junior adviser thirty years ago, shares his late master's resentment. As on many past occasions, the Federal Republic in 2013 stands accused of paying little regard to its European partners and of imposing an unpopular, stability-oriented monetary and fiscal policy across Europe. A further widening of Germany's economic lead over France intensifies the antagonism. During the dozen years since Schröder brought in economic reforms, coinciding with Merkel's accession to the chancellorship after the 2005 election, a sweeping reorganisation of the German economy has put France increasingly in the shade. For nearly a decade, and with just two exceptions (the 2009 recession, and in 2013), Germany's growth rate has outstripped France's every year. That is the longest period of above-average German expansion since the country's immediate post-war recovery sixty years ago. Germany's experience since the 2009 recession has hardly been stellar, but it has clearly exceeded that of France: in the five years between 2010–14, Germany's annual GDP growth was around 2 per cent, whereas France could manage only 1 per cent.

All this has increased French feelings of envy, frustration and (even) inferiority. Unlike Germany, it has highly active anti-euro parties, led by the Front National, which will make a renewed assault on the French presidency at the 2017 election – helping to drive the entirety of French politics sharply to the right. This is one of the reasons why Germany is extremely nervous about the possibility of Britain leaving the EU after the 2016–17 referendum. In view of the fluctuations in French politics, German leaders have good reason to recall Adenauer's cryptic statement to party colleagues in 1953 that Germany did not wish to be left alone in Europe with the 'more or less hysterical French'.[39] Under pressure from both left and right, Hollande has emphasised France's discomfort with German-style austerity, saying it will result in an 'explosion' in Europe's crisis countries.

France and Germany are poles apart in ideas on institutional renewal for the euro bloc. Traditionally, the French have always wished to create strong European institutions that can enforce dynamic growth, despite negative external influences. The German objective, especially at times of monetary upheaval, is to build strong institutions on the Bundesbank model, in order to protect Europe against inflation. The euro area is moving to implement more policy cohesion to compensate for the failings of the early years, but France and Germany are following different models. Germany's plans for economic governance are to establish a coordinating body to enact a common budgetary, fiscal, social and labour market policy, and so guarantee the euro's proper functioning. Hollande has made it clear that France wishes to set up an 'economic government', chaired by yet another semi-permanent president who would further swell the army of diverse European policy chiefs. This body would meet monthly to set (in some ill-defined way) economic, fiscal and social policy. A further element of the French plans is less explicit: this 'government' would probably be a kind of watchdog for the European Central Bank.

France is on the horns of a merciless dilemma. The best way to gain support for its ideas in Europe would be to lead a sub-bloc encompassing the other two big euro economies from the south, Italy and Spain. However, forming an overt grouping with what some call the 'Club Med' faction would fatally weaken France's ability to realise its prime ambition of operating on an equal footing with Germany. In a persistent euro stalemate, France is at the centre of the chess board.

14 The Bundesbank strikes back

THE GERMAN Bundesbank – which, during past skirmishes, was uncharitably termed in France the 'monster of Frankfurt' – has been cut down to size. The European Central Bank has taken over its mantle. The German central bank no longer forms the vital enterprise behind European money. But it constitutes the nexus in the past, present and future of Germany's unfinished drive to correct the continent's ever-present tendency towards disorder. After a series of setbacks, the Bundesbank has reinvented itself and is back in business as by far the most important central bank among the ECB's constituent shareholders. The Bundesbank no longer has the power to decide by itself – its leader has just one vote out of twenty-five on the ECB's decision-making council. It no longer has enough power to stop things happening – as was shown when it was unable to prevent the ECB moving to full-scale quantitative easing in March 2015. But it has sufficient clout to slow down developments and ensure that, whatever happens, ECB decision-making remains dogged by doubt and division – hardly a propitious background for resounding confidence in the euro's prospects.

The Bundesbank is now confronting expectations (and

constraints) that have never been greater. Jens Weidmann, the Bundesbank president since 2011, is a youthful, self-deprecating yet tough-minded counterweight to the dominance of Mario Draghi, the Italian ECB president. One of Weidmann's strengths is that, before his previous job as economic adviser to Angela Merkel (2006–11), he headed the Bundesbank's monetary policy department. This makes him one of the select few Bundesbank 'insiders' to ascend to the top post. The Bundesbank has rediscovered its central place in German decision-making, throwing its influence behind the often unsatisfactory compromises of implementing German sound-money principles across Europe. It represents a rallying point for opposition, in Germany and around Europe, to further bailouts for problem-hit southern countries that fail to respect the euro's formerly unheeded disciplines. And the Bundesbank crystallises the diverse pressures on Germany caused by fusing its money with eighteen other diverse countries, for whom previous experience of collisions with Germany in the military and monetary fields have clear repercussions on present-day crisis management.

The Bundesbank has a key role in managing the inherent conflicts of interest behind Germany's simultaneous desires for stable markets for its exports and inflation-free currency at home. The risks of extending credit to what Draghi himself calls the euro system's 'permanent debtors' are all on the Bundesbank's balance sheet. As a result of the progressive withdrawal of loans to the peripheral states by German commercial banks, the Bundesbank holds a sizeable proportion of Germany's much-increased net foreign assets of €1,400 billion. In the case of default or departure by the problem countries, the Bundesbank would shoulder a large share of the ensuing losses, which would then ultimately be borne by German taxpayers. The Bundesbank thus represents a trinity of forces: it forms the template for a European experiment that seeks to graft German success onto a much larger organism; it is the reproving voice behind constant entreaties for errant members to mend their ways or face dire consequences; and it is the repository of vast potential damage to Germany's financial strength should the adventure end in tears.

Around the world, in the years before monetary union, the Bundesbank's mix of self-righteousness, stubbornness and independence attracted fear and respect in equal measure. Monetary stability at home and in Europe were two sides of the same coin. But, as a succession of exchange rate crises in the European Monetary System in the 1980s and 1990s showed, maintaining the equilibrium became increasingly difficult. The Bundesbank's central place underpinned the system's strength, but blocked its reform. The Bundesbank was not a European institution: it was manifestly, irrefutably German. And for all these reasons, it had to be sacrificed on the altar of Maastricht. As Jacques Attali, François Mitterrand's international adviser, once confirmed, the Maastricht treaty was a complicated operation with a simple objective: to abolish the D-Mark.

After the euro's birth, the Bundesbank seemed to sink into oblivion. It was relegated to the status of executing other people's decisions. An Anglo-Saxon central bank governor who carried his own scars from past Bundesbank intransigence once proclaimed (not without malice) that the once-proud central bank should be renamed the 'Frankfurt branch' of the European Central Bank. With the escalation of the financial crisis after 2008, the traditional fault lines re-emerged. In a series of combative encounters over the ECB's support for weaker economies through purchases of their government bonds, the Bundesbank demonstrably became a minority within the euro club, first while Axel Weber was its president and then, after his resignation, with Weidmann at the helm. But it was a vocal minority. The collapse of the Bundesbank's old realm has been only apparent; in a different guise, the empire has struck back.

Weidmann recognises the risk of being outvoted under the one-person-one-vote rules of the ECB council (comprising the ECB directors and the heads of euro-area central banks; since 2011, the composition of the now twenty-five-strong council has shifted to include two women, Sabine Lautenschläger, the former Bundesbank deputy president who is now on the ECB executive board, and Chrystalla Georghadji, governor of the Central Bank of Cyprus). Arithmetically, the Bundesbank chief has the same voting weight as Malta's central bank president, even though Germany's economy is 400 times bigger. So Weidmann has taken the battle for sound money to the wider arena of politics and public opinion. The fragmentation of the European polity is a clear drawback to this undertaking, but Weidmann has one advantage: he can speak for 82 million Germans. The Bundesbank has lost none of its legendary support from the German population. As Jacques Delors once said: 'Not all Germans believe in God, but they all believe in the Bundesbank.' But, in addition to building up the Bundesbank's public relations activities in Germany, Weidmann has bolstered the Bundesbank's communications activities in the language of international financial markets – English. In the fractured field of European finance, Weidmann's message goes out loud and clear across international as well as domestic channels.

The Bundesbank has to use its influence with care. Three post-war chancellors – Ludwig Erhard, Kurt Georg Kiesinger and Helmut Schmidt – owe their political demise directly or indirectly to clashes with the central bank; however, it was defeated in its tussles with Helmut Kohl over German reunification and monetary union. The Bundesbank can win only if it chooses the battleground. Although the Bundesbank's status is one of quintessential independence, in practice its role is highly political, underlined by the circumstances under which two leading Bundesbankers retreated from the fray in 2011 after losing their policy-making hold. Weidmann's predecessor Axel Weber and Jürgen Stark, Germany's representative on the ECB's executive board (previously the Bundesbank's deputy president), both decided to quit after a series of disagreements that centred on the ECB's bond-market purchases. Weidmann, however, is taking a more sophisticated approach. He commands greater leverage in Berlin, and is highly unlikely to resign, preferring to fight his ground.

Weber and two other previous Bundesbank presidents, Karl Otto Pöhl and Ernst Welteke, left their jobs early, as a result of political intrigues. Weidmann has greater negotiating skills than either Weber or Stark. Some of his strictures – arguing against European debt mutualisation and for firmer controls over euro states seeking bailout funds – have become part of Merkel's own political vocabulary. He has remodelled the central bank into a more effective, longer-term fighting force. And he has opened up an operational partnership with Draghi under which both men, powerful and vulnerable in different ways, realise that they have no alternative but to forge an understanding – even if frequently they are condemned to disagree. This is a high-wire act of great complexity, and the outcome is uncertain. In 2012–15, Draghi appeared to win most of the battles. So Weidmann's task is to stay aloft for longer than anyone else – knowing that both he and the institution he leads face many more struggles.

15 In Italy, more showdowns

THE PROTEST vote in the Italian parliamentary elections of February 2013 was a deep setback for euro optimists. The message of the populists' victory contained many components: it signalled (unsurprising) displeasure with austerity; distaste for the political ruling classes; and desire for new faces at the helm. But more broadly, it was a vote against the country being led in a way that many Italians believed no longer benefits ordinary people. Italy will stumble on with one of the euro area's poorest records on growth, employment and structural change – a metaphor for the euro bloc's well-practised art of muddling through. Because of Italy's status as a founder member of the European Six that created the Common Market in the 1950s, Italy cannot be expelled from the euro and is very unlikely to leave of its own volition – a fundamental factor behind monetary union's unstable state of limbo.

The country that in many ways offers the most attractive living conditions of anywhere in Europe has registered substandard growth continuously for more than two decades. This reflects structural shortcomings in both the public and the private sector that pre-date the euro and that the new currency has done nothing to heal – or may even have made worse. After a messy period of wrangling, a coalition took power two months after the February 2013 vote, under an inoffensive left-of-centre politician, Enrico Letta. In a bloodless political coup in February 2014, Letta was replaced by a much more aggressive politician, again from the centre-left, Matteo Renzi, the thirty-nine-year-old mayor of Florence. Together with his experienced and wily finance mister, Pier Carlo Padoan, Renzi has introduced much-needed reforms in pensions and public services, and has been using as much budgetary flexibility as possible to relaunch the economy on a new path. It is too early to say whether Renzi's and Padoan's hitherto limited success signals a genuine turnaround in Letta's fortunes.

At the heart of the imbroglio is a disturbing paradox. The defeat in 2013 of the reformist technocrat prime minister, Mario Monti, was widely blamed on opposition to belt-tightening and restructuring. However, a succession of administrations (including Monti's) had failed to introduce anything like the degree of reform needed to put the Italian economy onto a longer-term stable footing and to guarantee the country's place in monetary union. Thoroughgoing steps are needed to improve business efficiency, build competitiveness, reshape the public sector and cut debt. The populace has launched a pre-emptive strike against radical measures that have never been taken.

In a reflection of the intractable nature of Italy's problems, none of those who led the field in the inconclusive poll outcome would declare himself either willing or able to lead the country. Beppe Grillo, a former comedian whose internet-based Five Star Movement was the real winner, claimed that his job was to go into opposition. Letta's government is composed of two parties that were bitter opponents before the vote: his left-wing Democratic Party and the conservative People of Freedom, led by discredited ex-prime minister and media mogul Silvio Berlusconi, who has taken an increasingly anti-euro and anti-German line in recent years. Disconcertingly, Pier Luigi Bersani, who led the Democratic Party until he resigned shortly after the election after failing to form a government, pointed out that 'only a madman' would take on the post of Italian prime minister.

Mario Monti, an economics professor and former European commissioner who is widely admired in Europe and the US for his scholarly tenacity, may be popular with the elites in Berlin and Washington, but he failed to win a foothold among the Italian people. Monti took command of an administration of non-elected officials in November 2011 after his predecessor, Berlusconi, was ousted in what amounted to an economic coup by the European Central Bank. In August 2011, ECB President Jean-Claude Trichet and Mario Draghi, then head of the Bank of Italy, demanded that Berlusconi toughen the country's austerity measures as a prerequisite for government bond purchases by the ECB. This forced Berlusconi into a humiliating climb-down.

As ECB President Draghi explained with undiplomatic bluntness a few weeks after the election, Italy has been economically on 'autopilot', in line with strictures from the European Union on lowering deficit and debt. Sooner or later, however, as Renzi recognises, economic policy will have to take on a more pro-growth bias that is more in line with the electorate's desires – with consequences that may upset the purveyors of European economic orthodoxy in Germany and elsewhere.

The most explosive impact of Italy's electoral tilt against economic rigour may be felt outside the country. It is not difficult to see in Paris, Rome and Madrid that an anti-austerity coalition is taking shape across the three other large euro economies outside Germany, a combination already endorsed by some German Social Democrat politicians.

Italy's difficulties in coming to terms with life inside the single currency were predictable enough. The hope of overcoming years of stagnation by introducing an irreversible currency peg with the Germans was, from the outset, an exceptionally ambitious one. In the late 1990s, the German government and the Bundesbank viewed Italian membership of monetary union with great scepticism. However, a series of short-term tax increases and spending cuts, as well as greatly reduced capital market interest rates, yielded the necessary budget deficit reduction for Italy to demonstrate sufficient convergence with the other Europeans. A sentimental attachment to Italy's experience as a founder member of the European Community, as well as fears that Italy could become super-competitive outside the euro bloc and thus damage the German economy, persuaded the Germans to accept Italy into monetary union.

The only European central bank chief who argued against his country's membership, Antonio Fazio, Draghi's predecessor as governor of the Bank of Italy, argued strongly against Italy joining the euro, on the grounds that Italian companies would rapidly lose their competitiveness under the constraints of a fixed exchange rate. In 2006, Fabrizio Saccomanni, then the Bank of Italy's director general, who in April 2013 took over the key post of economics and finance minister in the Letta government, told me: 'Although it is painful to admit for a central bank governor, Fazio felt we had to devalue from time to time to regain competitiveness and to support economic activity.'[40] Fazio subsequently faced long-drawn-out court appearances and judicial investigations over a 2005 banking scandal, but his judgement on Italy's participation in the euro proved correct. Many well-meaning Italian politicians and business leaders say that the only way to drag the country out of its chronic mess is to adjust to Germanic standards of competitive economic management. So far, Renzi and Padoan have achieved a measure of success, but a great deal more needs to be done. As Italy limps on from showdown to showdown, further dissonance between good intentions and adverse consequences lies ahead.

16 The reward of banking union

THERE ARE many potential advantages to combining Europe's regulations on banking and finance in order to produce harmonised governance structures for banks. Doing so would reduce the threat of financial flare-ups, restart credit flows to hard-up countries, and enable better services for consumers and businesses.

In mid-2012, European governments decided on far-reaching moves towards banking union. These measures appeared, in theory, sensible and necessary; and they have been put into effect far more quickly than seemed possible during the peak of the European debt crisis.

European banking union interferes with certain rights that governments regard – along with the power to tax and spend, and to go to war – as inalienable: the right to oversee banks' performance and to restructure or close them down when things go wrong. A secure, joined-up, efficient European banking system that safeguards the prosperity of Europe's citizens is a worthy goal. Overcoming the practical difficulties is a formidable task. Yet Europe can draw some satisfaction in having completed the challenge of bringing 123 of the largest banks in the euro area (comprising 82 per cent of overall banking assets) under the purview of joint supervisory teams from the European Central Bank and national banking supervisors in each of the member countries.

What might appear to be the easiest part of banking union – achieving effective, cross-border supervision – has proved to be technically and organisationally problematic, but achievable. Implementing the other two parts of banking union – setting up a single authority and a restructuring fund to wind up failed banks, and establishing Europe-wide deposit insurance – is still more difficult, and has opened up a Pandora's box of discord and wrangling. Germany plays a key role, not simply because of its status as the biggest economy and creditor, but also because roughly half of the euro area's 4,000-plus banks are German.

A banking union in Europe, designed to create the same kind of uniformity and flexibility displayed by banks in the US, has been under discussion for many years.[41] The idea was reactivated in 2012 for a specific reason – to channel funds from the European governments' European Stability Mechanism (ESM) rescue scheme in order to directly recapitalise problem banks in peripheral countries. The plan was to lower the strain on public finances in countries like Spain (which would otherwise have to find the money from government coffers) and so to hasten the return to growth and employment in Europe's struggling south. The aim is laudable: to break the vicious circle under which government action to stem banking crises automatically leads to ballooning public debt, higher interest rates, recession, defaults and more banking difficulties. Ending what the German government calls 'the destructive synergies between strained banks and indebted states' is a key priority for returning troubled euro countries to economic normality.

According to the 2012 strategy, direct recapitalisation was supposed to come into force as soon as Europe created a common set-up for cross-border banking supervision. However, as the flare-up over salvaging Cyprus in March 2013 demonstrated, the northern creditor countries' patience for direct public bank funding has been stretched to breaking point. Strengthening capital for banks in Spain, Ireland and Portugal will take place only under extremely restrictive conditions. The ESM will provide finance only after all other funding avenues – capital market issuance, creditor write-offs, shareholder contributions or forced losses by depositors – have been exhausted. Calling on taxpayers to rescue banks has become the exception rather than the rule.

In addition, the condition that banks can raise ESM funds only when European banking supervision is in place has proved more onerous than expected. The Maastricht treaty laid down a statutory path for cross-border supervision, allowing the European Central Bank to take responsibility for larger 'systemically important' banks, but many legal and technical hurdles remain. In taking over responsibility for supervision, the ECB has had to learn, somewhat belatedly, how to fulfil a function for which it was never equipped. It has recruited another 800 specialised staff (over and above its previous 1,600 employees) in the period up to 2015.

A further hurdle to cross has been the difficulty of setting up a Europe-wide resolution scheme for closing failed banks, which requires pan-European harmonisation of national insolvency and bankruptcy procedures, as well as a joint settlement fund to finance banks' restructuring. The German government has argued that a foolproof European resolution mechanism requires the time-consuming and wearisome step of amending the European treaties, a condition vehemently opposed by the European Commission and France. A legal study by the German government has concluded that, because of the diversity of national regulations, any attempt to drive through a Europe-wide system for winding-up banks on the basis of the present legal framework would be rejected in court judgments across the continent, resulting in huge political embarrassment and gigantic economic costs.

Still more obtrusive stumbling blocks line the way of the third component of banking union: establishment of a single deposit insurance system across Europe. The intention is to link up the European network of national deposit insurance funds, which already guarantees deposits of up to €100,000, so that the funding of national systems is not dependent on confidence in the credit standing of each country. The sums of money involved are enormous. German savings deposits are around €1.8 trillion – almost as much as the combined total for Italy, Spain, Ireland and Portugal. The Brussels plans for deposit insurance have been condemned in Germany as an attack on German savings and as an attempt at debt mutualisation through the back door. This makes it highly unlikely that the measure will be introduced in the next few years.

In all these considerations, it should be borne in mind that, for years before the euro's birth, central bankers, like many other observers, were clear that a monetary union and a single monetary policy could lead to moral hazard and economic overheating in some countries, and that this would be certain to bring overexpansion of credit and banking problems. But the politicians and technocrats behind the euro failed to put in hand any kind of preparations for its near-inevitable impact on the banking system. When the consequences did become apparent, the authorities reacted far too late. In most countries, the national central banks that make up the European Central Bank were responsible for banking supervision. They presided over grossly accelerated credit expansion in key countries – an expansion that stored up problems for later.

Recognising these lessons, the ECB has now been given much greater supervisory authority over a system that, at the beginning of monetary union, its constituent central banks grotesquely failed to control. The German Bundesbank has always held the view that combining monetary policy-setting and banking supervision under the roof of a single central bank is likely to lead to hazardous conflicts of interest by impeding tough decisions on anti-inflation credit-tightening. That remains its basic view – despite the strict separation that the ECB has established between its supervisory and monetary policy tasks.

So the true test of how well banking union is working will not come until the ECB needs to take tough decisions on raising interest rates. The person who has to deal with these conundrums is Danièle Nouy, the veteran French banking supervisor who took over as head of the supervisory board of the ECB's European single supervisory mechanism in 2014. For the time being, and as an inherent part of her job, she is broadcasting full confidence: 'We have completely grown into our role. The start of European supervision was an unprecedented task, but we are already a "game changer". Markets have more confidence in European banks than before. And let's not forget: Europe now has 1,000 additional banking supervisors. That alone should raise the quality of supervision.'[42]

17 The IMF's European conundrum

GERMANY AND Europe have manifestly failed to find the right approach to the role of the International Monetary Fund in various euro rescue operations. In late 2009 and early 2010, faced with the first signs of a looming economic storm in Greece, the German government and the ECB first tried to steer the IMF away from European involvement, on the misguided grounds that Europe could look after its own problems. The Fund was subsequently integrated into euro support actions, but has faced frustration about being co-opted into roles where it has often compromised on its principles of solid and sustainable financing.

Established at the end of the Second World War with the World Bank, as one of the two Bretton Woods institutions for a new age of peace, the Fund has not been able to develop a successful policy formula in Europe that combines the different tasks of providing technical assistance, injecting fresh money and policing economic policy conditionality. Meanwhile, the large emerging market economies that are playing a growing role in IMF governance are making plain their dissatisfaction with the size of the Fund's commitment to Europe. Not unreasonably, they are demanding that one of the wealthiest regions of the world show more self-reliance. In its conflict-strewn relationship with the Europeans, the IMF is performing a risky balancing act that worries many influential people in Washington and beyond and that satisfies no one. Instead of helping to propel the world economy into a new period of cooperation and consensus, monetary union has become a catalyst for increasing intercontinental alienation.

The Fund's deepening involvement in the European morass stands in contrast to its global orientation, with its 188 member countries (five fewer than the United Nations). Its large-scale lending to rich developed nations, with far less onerous conditions than those imposed on states in Asia during that continent's financial crisis of 1997–98, has attracted virulent complaints from developing countries that the Fund applies double standards. Its relationships with large emerging market countries such as China, India, Brazil and Russia have come under strain. Unfortunately, in view of the stalled state of European affairs, the Fund can neither engineer a decisive breakthrough nor extricate itself from the debt quagmire.

Rather than withdraw from loans to Greece, as it hoped to do in 2013–14, the Fund finds itself caught up in a fresh war of nerves over participating in the €86 billion European-led bail-out for Greece agreed in August 2015. Fund officials as well as Greek politicians know that Greece cannot repay on time. And its massive existing loans (amounting to around 190 per cent of GDP in 2015, and due to rise to 200 per cent in 2016) are owed mainly to official creditors abroad – so the money is needed largely to repay existing liabilities rather than to plough into productive investment to revitalise the economy after years of belt-tightening and recession. The IMF has made clear that it will take part in fresh lending to Athens only if European politicians grant large-scale debt restructuring – a certain guarantee of friction between Washington and European capitals (especially Berlin) as negotiations start in 2016.

The adversarial nature of the Fund's European lending engagements poses a clear threat to its nearly seventy-year-old image as an independent world authority and monetary policeman. Adversity in Europe has claimed many victims; they include the IMF's own reputation and credibility.

In salvage missions for Greece, Ireland, Portugal, Spain and Cyprus, the IMF has broken ground in many ways, nearly all of them negative. It arrived unbidden on the scene in 2010, having been as disastrously unprepared for the crisis as the other members of the so-called 'troika' – the European Central Bank and the European Commission. As European economists analysing IMF actions in Europe put it:

In their surveillance work during the period 1999–2009, IMF staff never raised the possibility of major sovereign or balance-of-payment crises in the euro area, despite their intimate knowledge of crises elsewhere and potential parallels with the euro area that should have drawn their attention.[43]

Representatives of developing countries record how the IMF, along with western finance ministries and central banks, frequently told them that balance of payments crises could occur with the likes of Korea, Mexico and Argentina – but not with the Europeans.

The Fund had to see off German Finance Minister Wolfgang Schäuble's initial quixotic suggestion of a European Monetary Fund to provide financial support to countries like Greece, in a way that would show solidarity with France and demonstrate European independence from Washington. This singularly ill-timed proposal was eventually quashed when Europe collectively realised that it had no substitute for the IMF's technical resources and experience. But that it gained any traction at all demonstrated the mutual shallowness of understanding between the Fund and Europe.

The IMF's record in helping to run euro rescue programmes has been convoluted and unhappy – an experience shared by the other members of an increasingly dysfunctional troika. Because of the unusual macroeconomic circumstances – a requirement to keep the nominal exchange rate stable and to maintain (apart from in Cyprus) complete freedom of capital flows (not a feature of most previous IMF adjustment measures) – the falls in demand and output in the programme countries and the rises in unemployment were much greater than in the past. Rather than being in control, the IMF has had to submit to wildly fluctuating consequences of political decisions in different recipient states, ranging from the Dublin government's calamitous blanket guarantee for Irish bank liabilities (September 2008) to the Franco-German government accord imposing losses on private subscribers to peripheral country bonds (October 2010) and the ill-starred 2012 postponement of bank restructuring in Cyprus. The IMF has suffered the indignity of seeing its forecasts for economic growth and debt sustainability repeatedly blown off course. European recovery measures that have been delayed, half-hearted, poorly implemented or wrong-headed (sometimes all four) have frequently led to embarrassing about-turns and time-consuming renegotiations. The most spectacular episode (and the one most damaging to IMF credibility) was the Greek debt restructuring in February 2012, by far the biggest sovereign bankruptcy in history, which followed months of ever more threadbare denials. In June 2013, the IMF published a fiercely self-critical report – which itself led to a war of words with the European Commission – on how it and the EU handled Greece's 2010 bailout, saying growth assumptions were too optimistic and debt restructuring should have occurred much earlier.[44] Confirming the allegations made by IMF insiders at the time of the bailout, the report said the rescue went ahead even though Greece did not meet one of the IMF's main criteria for such a programme, namely that it had any chance of medium-term debt sustainability.

During its European involvement, the IMF has been beset by internal rivalries between factions that have pleaded either for softer or for more stringent policies towards errant European states. The hawkish faction – dubbed 'the ayatollahs' by some European negotiators – demonstrably gained ground during the Cyprus loan wrangling in March 2013. For two years, the IMF had agonised over whether a tough approach from Washington would push the euro bloc over the brink. But by spring 2013, senior Fund officials reasoned that the Europeans had at last built sufficient 'firewalls', so that a possible Cypriot euro exit would not force other states to follow suit. This enabled the IMF to unleash a new hard-line policy previously kept under wraps.

The Fund's hard-headed stance has been prompted by the promotion of more realistic and competent officials to run its European department. Another important factor has been the arrival as IMF managing director of Christine Lagarde, following the enforced departure in May 2011 of Dominique Strauss-Kahn, over an alleged sex offence. The swashbuckling economist-dealmaker had severely overstretched the Fund in lending to Greece. His blatant overruling of the Fund's own lending guidelines had been designed partly to burnish his political reputation ahead of a planned attempt to win the French presidential election. Unlike her predecessor, Lagarde, another previous French finance minister, but a lawyer rather than an economist, has heeded the IMF's expert staff and has paid far more attention to scepticism over European lending from China, India and other developing nations.

Both Strauss-Kahn and Lagarde have signally failed to resolve a festering dispute at the centre of monetary union, which focuses on responsibility for reducing current and capital account imbalances between deficit and surplus countries. The question is whether disequilibrium should be amended in an 'asymmetrical' fashion (that is, through painful measures to reduce demand in the deficit countries) or through 'symmetrical' means (whereby both surplus and deficit countries take simultaneous action). Adjustment in the euro bloc has been accomplished at the cost of great hardship in deficit nations, while those in surplus, above all Germany, have done comparatively little. Just as in the 1960s and 1970s, when the issue first came internationally to the surface, the Germans reject as inflationary any action to force down their high current account surplus, saying the onus for correction must remain with the deficit countries. Here, as in other areas, Europe is caught in the groove of history, relentlessly borne back towards the past. Breaking out and forging ahead remains a distant hope.

18 Anglo-Saxon ambivalence

US CONCERN over European woes runs deep. Ironic though it may be for a structure designed to foster stability, the euro bloc has become officially designated as the prime source of global economic risk, with wide-ranging implications for America's financial and business interests around the world. On the other hand, the US response to Europe's travails is not entirely free from duplicity. The Americans call repeatedly for Europe to show clear thinking and to enact speedy measures to end the malaise. In reality, the US has no strong interest in a radical solution to the euro crisis, nor any expectation that it will actually happen. A euro assailed by doubt and indecision, permanently and uncertainly poised between the extremes of teetering over the abyss and breaking through to a better future, may be unsatisfactory in many ways; but it makes the dollar look stronger and more solid. On the world stage, the Americans can deflect attention from their domestic economic woes with a display of statesmanlike dominance and crisis-management assurance. The euro's problems maintain intact America's so-called 'exorbitant privilege', under which it can issue the dollar as the leading reserve currency to finance home-grown budget and payments deficits by importing capital from foreigners. The euro's troubles will not be solved, but they will remain sufficiently under control to avoid a full-scale world-wide financial collapse. For President Barack Obama, the Federal Reserve and the big American banks and industrial groups, a combination of European paralysis and American superiority is not an entirely negative scenario.

There is necessarily less distance and more directness in Britain's approach to the currency stalemate. The UK is the euro bloc's leading trade partner, ahead of the US and China; in 2012, it moved ahead of France as the country with which Germany does most trade; even though the growth of German trade in recent years has mainly been with non-EU countries, Germany is still heavily dependent on its traditional economic links closer to home – and this includes the UK. Turbulence in the euro area automatically weakens the British economy. So Prime Minister David Cameron's Conservatives, like the opposition Labour Party, regularly call for major economic reforms on the continent and for a move to some form of political union (however defined), in which Britain, of course, would never participate.

This concept forms part of the bedrock of Cameron's negotiating position over the terms of a renegotiated settlement between the UK and the European Union that will be put to the British electorate in a referendum in 2016 or 2017. As part of a change in the relationship between Britain and the rest of Europe, the UK government wishes the EU to agree that the Union should be a 'multicurrency bloc' in which non-euro member countries such as Britain should be able to maintain their own currencies (in this case, sterling) without impediment, and in particular without interfering with the rules of the European single market. This proposal looks entirely legitimate in view of the likelihood that other significant members of the EU (notably Poland, Sweden, Denmark, the Czech Republic and Hungary) will almost certainly wish to keep their own currencies and stay outside the euro for several years to come.

Cameron's basic negotiating position on the euro is backed by logic: extending the purely monetary rules of the single currency union is in line with precepts put forward by many European governments over the past twenty years. Constant repetition of a plan in which Britain does not believe and which is highly unlikely to be put into effect confers upon the British a comforting air of intellectual rigour and moral superiority that would otherwise be out of reach.

As with the US, Britain's de facto position with respect to the euro is more satisfactory than it might appear at first sight. There are four reasons why the euro crisis provides Britain with a margin of political and economic benefit. First, the euro's structural weaknesses make sterling stronger on currency markets than would otherwise be the case (however incongruous that may appear, given the UK's own economic problems). A firmer pound does wreak some damage on British exports, by lowering UK competitiveness on foreign markets; but this disadvantage is offset by other positive factors, such as Britain's ability to issue larger volumes of relatively low-interest government bonds to foreign investors, and enhanced international purchasing power for British importers and travellers abroad.

Second, continental Europe's weakness gives the British somewhat greater possibilities to exhibit independence and self-reliance in debates about Europe's future. There is no denying the wisdom of the decision not to enter the euro in the late 1990s and early 2000s. According to Gus O'Donnell, formerly head of Britain's civil service and a member of the UK Treasury team that formulated the view that Britain should stay outside the single currency, 'Over the last few years as the Greek crisis has unfolded I have lost count of the number of times that I have thanked God that the UK is not a member of the euro.'[45] Politically, Cameron's decision to call a referendum on UK EU membership has backfired, to the extent that many in the Conservative Party are implacably opposed to Britain's adherence and will vote against it irrespective of the government's negotiating success. As John Major, a previous Tory prime minister, once said, 'Europe is a wolf coming up the path to devour the Conservative Party.' Cameron is undoubtedly in a fragile position. However, given near-perpetual Conservative wrangling over Europe, his hand is made somewhat stronger by the poor state of the European economy and of the Franco-German relationship, which has made the Berlin government, German business and other parts of the EU anxious to keep the UK in the EU – although clearly not at any price.

Third, and linked to the overall question of Britain's place in Europe, endless uncertainty about the outcome of the single currency experiment relieves the pressure on Britain to make a final decision on its relationship with the euro bloc. If, in coming years, fundamentally pro-European and relatively well-run EU countries such as Poland, Sweden or Denmark were to decide to join a successful euro, Britain's position outside would appear far more isolated and perhaps ultimately untenable. This would be an excruciating dilemma for the current or any future British government. In fact, as a consequence of years of euro attrition, and in view of the prospect of more to come, none of these countries are likely to become members over the next ten years. Any decision to join the euro bloc would require these countries' well-founded scepticism about the governance and performance of the euro to be overcome and for a referendum to be held in each country. So Britain can, in good conscience and in good company, remain outside.

Fourth, whatever the ructions in the Conservative Party, Britain's domestic political constellation would be more unstable if Europe were in a better state. Europe's weakness made possible the establishment of the Conservative–Liberal Democrat coalition after the 2010 parliamentary elections; an alliance between the pro-European Liberals and Eurosceptic Tories was only realisable because Europe's unattractiveness lowered the likelihood that the Liberals and the Conservatives would find themselves on a collision course over ties with the continent. (In the 2015 election, the Conservatives emerged with sufficient parliamentary seats to rule without a coalition.) Perhaps even more important, Europe's shortcomings, increasing the Scots' hesitancy about an independent Scotland joining the EU and the euro, helped tilt the balance towards a 'No' against Scottish independence in the 2014 referendum. An inverse relationship seems clear: European strains improve British cohesiveness.

The contradictory, double-edged tone to Anglo-American

views on the euro project has a long tradition. Both Britain's relationship with the other European countries and its attitude to the basic goal of European integration have always been subject to doubt and have been tinged with an air of schizophrenia. Despite much-expanded trade and investment with the continent since Britain joined the European Community in 1973, Winston Churchill's 1944 epigram remains valid: as he confided to Charles de Gaulle, whenever the UK had to decide between the US and Europe, it would, for strategic reasons, invariably choose 'the open sea'. Anglo-Saxon attitudes on European monetary matters have fluctuated sporadically, yet persistent scepticism is the underlying common denominator. In 1971, at a time of European vexation over a weak dollar and lax US fiscal and monetary policy, President Richard Nixon's treasury secretary, John Connally, brusquely told the Europeans: 'The dollar may be our currency, but it's your problem.' Four decades later, the positions are reversed. This time the Europeans themselves have provided the world with the currency that has sent out waves of global instability. Persistent in their ambivalence, reluctant to undertake any kind of advance commitment in case it harms their interests, yet ready to act if the flows reach new shores, the Anglo-Saxons are watching which way the tides run.

19 Asia's star rises

NOT SINCE the Second World War and the fall of Singapore to the Japanese army in 1942 has Europe's star sunk so low in the east. Asian policy-makers have greeted the clash of civilisations and cultures in the euro bloc with stunned incomprehension. The plan for building Europe's global status held particular resonance for the countries in the vanguard of world economic growth. In 1999, the euro appeared to many Asian central banks – especially to the Chinese and Japanese, the world's No. 2 and No. 3 economies, with the largest currency reserves – as an instrument of economic salvation, an alternative to the monopoly power of the dollar as the main international reserve currency, and a beacon of hope for a new world economic order. But reality has lagged far behind ambition. Asia's previous tendency to look to Europe for a lead in enhancing economic and political integration has been replaced by disappointment and displeasure at the Europeans' uncanny ability to lose control of a project designed to secure their destiny.

The goal was to give the world economic community access to an alternative currency that would rival the dollar in attractiveness and reliability. A new European pioneering spirit would open up fresh trading and investment relationships of immense benefit to Asia and would boost its weight in the world economy. Some aspects of that vision can still hold true. To escape the European mire, companies across the continent have greatly increased their trade with Asia. But the illusion has been dashed that the euro would develop as a genuine counterpart to the dollar.

The tarnishing of Europe's image extends well beyond matters of money. The Chinese, Japanese, Koreans and the Southeast Asian countries believed they had started to understand Europe. When the European currency arrived, they invested in it with eagerness and alacrity, believing that, before long, some form of European state entity would arise to add essential backing. When, fifteen years later, Asians look at the map of Europe, they still see a maze of provinces and principalities of indeterminate loyalty, inconsequential leadership and uneven performance. The euro exists in the balance sheets of Asian central banks, sovereign funds, companies and asset managers, but the European state they thought would stand behind it remains an obscure cipher.

In a sense, Europe's misfortunes have served up a salutary reality check. The Asians, at home in an amorphous continent of swirling diversity that is considerably more heterogeneous than Europe, have never developed concrete plans for an Asian currency, but they saw Europe as a template for possible action. After the European debacle, Europe has slid precipitously down the league table of role models. The prospects for any kind of Asian currency appear even more distant. Asia is making efforts to increase trade integration, harmonise financial markets and improve regional monetary cooperation, partly to build up financial safety nets as an alternative to the IMF. Governments across the continent know that the key to any kind of monetary experiment is to achieve consensus in politics, which – in view of Asia's myriad disputes and rivalries – is a long way from being established. The European experience has shown the acute dangers of putting the monetary cart before the political horse. A leading Far East central bank official says, 'We have always thought that the Europeans have better systems and better people. Now there is serious doubt whether this is really true.'

More generally, the inscrutable Asians gaze upon the indecipherable Europeans with incredulity, if not contempt. In private, policy-makers bring a litany of charges against the European elite, accusing it of 'arrogance', 'incompetence' and 'not getting it'. Asia's initial inclination at the onset of the European crisis to intervene directly, through purchases of individual countries' government bonds, has given way to a marked reluctance to get too deeply involved. The Greek sovereign bankruptcy in 2012 was a shock; the Asians were told it could never happen. Even if the big central banks and sovereign funds continue to amass bond issues of the European bailout fund, they do so without much enthusiasm. The Chinese have no desire to see the euro collapse, because Europe forms China's largest global export market, and a euro that is over-weak against the renminbi would harm Chinese companies' competitiveness. But the Chinese desire to shore up the euro will decrease in coming years, in light of the international rise of the renminbi – recognised formally by the IMF as a reserve currency at the end of 2015 – and changes in China's economic structure towards less reliance on exports and more on domestically driven growth. Like the Germans with the D-Mark in the 1960s, the Chinese may come to see the advantages of a strong domestic currency.

Leading Asians show disdain for Europe's lack of resolve, coordination, flexibility and staying power in healing its self-inflicted wounds. By contrast, they say, in their own relatively rapid recovery from the financial crisis of 1997–98, Asian countries amply displayed those very features. One well-connected Chinese financier points out that, during the Asian crisis, Koreans sold gold to help the government; meanwhile the Greeks go on strike. He underlines the fact that China is not expecting Europe dramatically to increase its higher value imports from China and adds that the entire basis of trade and investment ties with the Europeans needs to be restructured: 'We export a lot of labour-intensive products, we get dollars in return, we buy European bonds, and they decline. We'd be better off investing in developing countries' infrastructure or buying high-tech European companies.'

Already officially enshrined as bankers to the world's biggest debtor, the US, the Chinese have no wish to become a last-ditch lender to the Europeans. Like other large investors throughout Asia, the Chinese are surprised that travelling European policy-makers not infrequently ask them to buy bonds from European governments, when the institution they expected to be the lender of last resort – the European Central Bank – balks (for whatever reason) at carrying out the same role. The Beijing government is under pressure from an alert internet-savvy public to resist cash appeals when millions of ordinary Chinese are struggling with worrisome social, economic and environmental conditions.

Cartoons in the *People's Daily* show a plump European trying to gobble up the lunch of a skinny Chinese. In a quaintly Biblical reference, the official Xinhua news agency rules out the idea that emerging market economies should play a 'Good Samaritan' role towards the feckless Europeans.

As the fulcrum of world money and finance shifts slowly eastwards, Asian monetary authorities have no wish to bank fully on the dollar or the euro. The future lies in internationalising Asian currencies – including the yen and the renminbi – in trade and investment, and in enhancing regional cooperation to reduce dependence on the west. Many leading Asian central banks have to deal with the politically sensitive issue of making annual net losses on their western currency holdings. The central banks of China, Indonesia, Malaysia, South Korea and Thailand are building up reserve holdings of each other's currencies. Growing European trade with Asia – in 2012, Germany generated 17 per cent of total trade with Asia, against only 12 per cent in 1999 – is promoting Asian currency internationalisation. Shanghai, Beijing, Singapore, Hong Kong and Tokyo (as well as other centres, such as Seoul, Bombay, Kuala Lumpur, Jakarta and Bangkok) are building up their importance for international banks and asset managers. Asian savings are increasingly being invested in the region, rather than being diverted to London, Frankfurt or New York. The contours of a more integrated Asian economic and financial area are emerging. Asia will become more preoccupied with its own development and less interested in helping the Europeans resolve their tangle of muddle and fiasco. As Europe's star sinks, Asia's shines more brightly.

20 War and peace

INTERNAL AND external paralysis is systematically reducing the Old Continent's strategic relevance. The geopolitical worries with which Europe had to wrestle in 2015 are compounding the Old Continent's agony. Europe's under-skilled and over-stretched politicians will not hew quickly through the Gordian knot. Indecision and self-isolation are likely to feed off each other: a self-perpetuating retreat. Higher-growth areas of the world, rather than fruitlessly calling for Europe to resolve its woes in the interests of the international community, will simply sidestep the euro crisis and leave the bloc to resolve its difficulties in its own time. They may have to wait for a while.

The major economic powers of the US, China and Japan will not press for radical euro healing measures that could destabilise financial markets by forcing real decisions, for example on whether certain countries should leave. The big economies have no interest in provoking a financial market firestorm that would lead to a destabilising appreciation of their own currencies and hamper the faltering world economic recovery. Like Shakespeare's Macbeth, all participants are 'in blood stepp'd in so far' that a return to national currencies would be a journey of horror. So muddling through is the preferred option, inside and outside Europe. One important variant can certainly be excluded. Other parts of the world have been so irritated and frustrated by Europe's inability to resolve its difficulties, and have so little confidence that any breakthrough is on the horizon, that significant direct financial support from other large economies can be ruled out.

Europe could take the initiative, for example by deciding on a significant increase in assistance for debtor countries, or by dividing the currency bloc between northern and southern countries. The former option would open the way to a European transfer union by pooling official European debt; Greek debt restructuring in 2016 would mark a further step in this direction. This step is hotly contested by German political and public opinion (and the constitutional court), but may be on the way, although in a stealthy fashion that will be resisted at every step and could take place on a sustained basis only if accompanied by centralised controls on countries' economic policies.

The latter step could lead to a more appropriate and stable performance of the reconfigured component currencies of monetary union. But before that happened, a period of European monetary chaos would probably ensue, dealing a serious blow to national economies. So this, too, is unlikely to come about in the shorter term. Helmut Kohl once termed monetary union 'a matter of war and peace'. His description was apt. Debtors and creditors are locked in political-psychological limbo, neither full-scale war nor durable peace. They are hemmed in by mutual blockades, reminiscent of Jean-Paul Sartre's existentialist play

Huis clos (No Way Out), in which three people are condemned to remain in a locked room for eternity.

Germany, as the powerhouse and centrepiece of Europe, faces a task of gargantuan proportions. Since the Second World War, it has successfully given equal weight to apparently opposing objectives: simultaneous partnership with Europe and the US; political settlement with France and the Soviet Union; equilibrium between the dollar and the D-Mark; joint solidarity with the Europeans and its own citizens. All have been maintained, at times through feints and compromise. This time it is different. The two objectives of domestic and European stabilisation, which used to run in parallel, are proceeding along divergent lines. Germany has not undergone the historical conditioning to make hard choices to overcome the challenge; the boldest hope of crisis managers like Angela Merkel is simply to survive.

The precedents are not compellingly positive. The tipping points of German history have often been generated by fatal misjudgements about Germany's capabilities and vulnerabilities, coinciding with yawning gaps between external perception and internal reality. A perfect symbol of the Germans' innate contradictions: whenever foreigners consider them strong, they are weak, and vice versa. Napoleon III catastrophically underestimated the power of Prussia in 1870, ushering in the German Empire. In 1918, on the collapse of the western front, and then throughout the Weimar Republic, the extent of German fragility was not recognised abroad. After 1933, foreign observers consistently played down the growing military might of the Nazi Reich. After the Second World War, a defeated and dismembered Germany, deprived of sovereignty, defence forces and foreign exchange, looked vulnerable, but the economic weaklings were the western victor powers. During and after reunification, many foreigners (two prominent examples being Margaret Thatcher and François Mitterrand) overestimated the Germans' strength, even though it was temporarily crumbling as Helmut Kohl piled on the policy mistakes in absorbing East Germany. In the early 2000s, as Gerhard Schröder prepared to launch his reform policy, many wrote Germany off as a brittle giant, just as it was girding its loins for the future. During the euro's troubles, partner countries have looked to the Germans as a source of boundless redemption, not realising the thin line separating European salvation from financial overstretch.

As a land of economic robustness, surrounded by neighbours in various degrees of infirmity, Germany adds greatly to Europe's heterogeneity. But the Germans do not have the power of action to end the crisis in either a positive or a negative way. The reality that monetary union has strengthened more than it has weakened Germany is now generally recognised; but the country is at risk from other states which feel threatened by the new-found German robustness. The first chancellor of the German Empire, Otto von Bismarck, like the first leader of the post-war rump state, Konrad Adenauer, feared the 'nightmare of coalitions' – destructive rivalries against bands of insecure neighbours. Such anxieties are re-entering the political lexicon of Berlin's present-day leaders.

Oscillating perceptions of German strength provide a pattern, too, for the six different development phases that monetary union has hitherto traversed. In 1998–2003, we had the build-up, coinciding with the first president of the European

Central Bank, Wim Duisenberg, who had a hard time coping with the might of the dollar and the scepticism of financial markets. The second stage, a period of consolidation, ensued after November 2003, with the appointment of Duisenberg's successor, Jean-Claude Trichet, who had to endure occasional tussles with member governments over their efforts to rewrite monetary union's fiscal rules. The third phase was a period of defiance, as the euro strengthened and Trichet betrayed overconfidence by proclaiming himself 'Mr Euro'. This stage also featured irresponsibility and negligence as the ECB paid insufficient heed to growing euro imbalances. The fourth phase, from 2007, was one of premature triumph, as the euro bloc appeared to surmount the financial crisis more or less unscathed, and Trichet, too quick to exult over his tormentors, accused the euro's critics of foolish pessimism. With the first revelations of Greek misconduct in late 2009, we enter the fifth stage, the crisis period, which gave way in 2011 to the sixth, 'blame game' phase, when the different actors sidestep responsibility for the mishaps by indulging in ever-widening mutual recrimination. Further developments depend more on what happens in France, Italy and Spain than on what occurs in Greece or Germany. If things go unexpectedly well, the euro will embark on a seventh phase of healing. If they go badly wrong, the seventh phase will be called liquidation.

A ten-point plan to underpin the bloc for the longer term

To forestall unpleasant consequences for Europe, the euro member states could commit to the following action:

1.   Take binding steps to set up a full-scale political union with a centralised finance ministry, treasury and other governmental authorities, headed by a directly elected president accountable to the European Parliament. Voting strength would be in proportion to each country's economic weight, and an appropriate degree of power-sharing would be introduced in a federal system with national governments, in a bid to convince citizens that power was not being transferred too far away from national democratic control.

2.   Impose centralised European control of all member states' budgets and general economic policy, including the establishment of a Brussels- or Luxembourg-based Independent Budget and Debt Authority (linked to a European finance ministry and treasury) to set binding rules for euro bloc government spending and revenues and to check private sector credit growth.

3.   Transform the structure of the European Central Bank, so that it is owned by the governments – not the central banks – of countries that agree permanently to remain members of the euro; change the names of national central banks and turn them into branches of the European Central Bank in different countries; and transform the ECB into a lender of last resort for European governments, with voting power on decisions that is proportionate to individual states' gross domestic product or net creditor positions.

4.   Introduce a direct revenue-raising mechanism for

European Union organisations as part of an initiative to increase the centralised euro bloc budget.

5. Lay down clear, multi-year procedures for leaving and joining monetary union; bring in new arrangements for European states outside monetary union (or those that choose to leave it) to allow them to remain part of the European single market and a wider European Community.[46]

6. Introduce eurobonds for bloc-wide public sector borrowing under joint governmental credit guarantees.

7. Delay any new membership of monetary union until the above procedures have been agreed and a full independent analysis of the euro bloc's past developments and setbacks hitherto has been made; this could be linked to a public inquiry along the lines of a 'Truth and Reconciliation Commission' to shed light on what has gone wrong and how matters can be rectified.

8. Improve burden-sharing, so that the current account surplus countries agree to stimulate their economies and increase inflation rates to raise demand for exports from nations under stress.

9. Enact Marshall Plan-type aid flows for countries that fall seriously behind general euro bloc living standards – provided they fully meet centrally decided economic reform programmes.

10. Create further momentum behind a full-scale banking union for euro members, with supervision, resolution and deposit insurance secured by centralised European institutions underpinned by taxpayers.

This is a demanding list. And for the reasons made clear in this book, the plan is unrealisable. The most toxic contradiction in the single currency conundrum is this: the most necessary instrument to resolve the euro crisis – further European political and economic integration – has simultaneously been made unrealisable by European electorates' crisis-induced distrust of any steps to take decision-making and control further away from the people. As Nigel Lawson, the former British chancellor of the exchequer (who in 2015 became leader of the campaign for the UK to reject EU membership in the planned referendum), puts it, a nation state and its national currency work because the people feel that it is their country. 'This is partly a result of democracy – essentially the power of the people to sack the government – but it is also, and equally important, because there is a popular sense of national solidarity. There is no corresponding popular sense of European solidarity; the reverse has occurred.'[47]

So a broad master plan is unfeasible; even a watered-down version would be possible only for a smaller number of member states than there are at present, and they would need economic and political structures similar to those of Germany. A smaller monetary union would be much more stable than the existing design, but progress to this objective is hazardous, since no one knows whether the risks of contagion for other euro countries are manageable. So breaking through to a more settled system will be fraught with danger and difficulty.

Past negligence, present shortcomings, and failure to agree future responsibilities make a grand new beginning highly unlikely in the next few years. The euro will continue to exist:

in the coming period of an internationalising renminbi and yen, it may no longer be a truly global currency, but it will be more than merely a regional one. Because the consequences are universally feared, the nightmare of a total euro collapse will be avoided, yet deadlock and discord will linger on. In the course of time, and after some hardships, the euro may even become more stable: intact, but narrower and less ambitious. Intoxicated by the dream of combining money and power, Europe expected to bestride the world stage. In fact, as the curtain rises on a new age of western humility, it is stepping aside to make room for others.

Notes

1. Mark Rutte, interview with international news organisation, *Financial Times*, 27 November 2015.
2. George Orwell, *Nineteen Eighty-Four*, Secker & Warburg, London, 1949.
3. Otmar Issing, *Handelsblatt*, 20 October 2015.
4. Mario Draghi, speech, Helskini, 27 November 2014.
5. J.A. Schumpeter, *Das Wesen des Geldes*, Vandenhoeck u. Ruprecht, Göttingen, 1970, p.1.
6. Helmut Kohl, speech, Jouy-en-Josas, 3 December 1991.
7. Gerhard Schröder, conversation with author, Berlin, 26 April 2007.
8. Michael Stürmer, *Das ruhelose Reich, Deutschland 1866–1918*, Severin und Siedler, Berlin, 1983.
9. Heinrich Heine, *Englische Fragmente*, 1828.
10. Hans Tietmeyer, speech, Aachen, 3 November 1997.
11. Wilhelm Nölling, *Unser Geld – Der Kampf um die Stabilität der Währungen in Europa*, Ullstein, Berlin/Frankfurt, 1993, pp. 161–2.
12. Jean-Claude Trichet, speech, Frankfurt, 3 June 2008.
13. Guillermo de la Dehesa, *A Self-Inflicted Crisis? Design and management failures leading to the eurozone crisis*, Occasional Paper 86, Group of Thirty, Washington, D.C., 2012, available at: http://www.group30.org/images/PDF/ReportPDFs/OP86.pdf
14. 'Strong euro hid crisis, says EU chief', *Financial Times*, 14 June 2010.
15. Mario Draghi speech, Rome, 6 May 2013.
16. André Szász, conversation with author, December 2010.
17. Otmar Issing, *Der Euro: Geburt – Erfolg – Zukunft*, Vahlen, Munich, 2008, pp. 185–6.
18. European Commission, *EMU@10: Successes and challenges after ten years of Economic and Monetary Union*, 2008, available at: http://ec.europa.eu/economy_finance/publications/publication12682_en.pdf
19. European Commission, Economic and Financial Affairs, 'Myths and facts: Is it true…?', 30 April 2009, available at: http://ec.europa.eu/economy_finance/emu10/myths_en.htm
20. European Commission, Economic and Financial Affairs, 'Myths and facts', 30 April 2009, available at: http://ec.europa.eu/economy_finance/emu10/facts8_en.htm

21. Jacques Delors, speech, Brussels, 28 March 2012.
22. See, for example, Jean-Claude Trichet speeches in Hamburg, 13 May 2004; Amsterdam, 10 October 2004; Zurich, 30 March 2006; London, 29 November 2006; Frankfurt, 15 April 2008; Brussels, 16 May 2008; Munich, 10 July 2008.
23. Peter Praet, speech, Frankfurt, 15 June 2012.
24. Vítor Constâncio, speech, Athens, 23 May 2013.
25. Mario Draghi, speech, London, 26 July 2012.
26. Mario Draghi, speech, Shanghai, 3 June 2013.
27. Mario Draghi, statement at a press conference, Frankfurt, 7 August 2014.
28. Karl Otto Pöhl, conversation with author, Frankfurt, 29 June 1989.
29. ECB analysis on household wealth, 9 April 2013.
30. Jeroen Dijsselbloem, interview, Reuters, 25 March 2013, available at: http://uk.reuters.com/article/2013/03/25/uk-eurogroup-cyprus-dijsselbloem-idUKBRE92O0IL20130325
31. Athanasios Orphanides, lecture, Brussels, 13 June 2015, expanded in 'The euro area crisis five years after the original sin', MIT, Social Science Research Network Electronic Paper Collection, October 2015.
32. Edouard Balladur, Le Monde, 21 August 1992.
33. Ottmar Issing, remarks at conference, Hamburg, November 2007.
34. George Soros, 'Germany's choice', Project Syndicate website, 9 April 2013, available at: http://www.project-syndicate.org/commentary/a-simple-solution-to-the-euro-crisis-by-george-soros
35. Laurent Fabius, conversation with author, Paris, December 2010.
36. Otmar Emminger, letter to Johann-Baptist Schöllhorn, Frankfurt, 23 December 1970.
37. Karl Otto Pöhl, remarks to Bundesbank council, Frankfurt, May 1981.
38. Elisabeth Guigou, Une femme au cœur de l'Etat, Fayard, Paris, 2000, p. 77.
39. Hans-Peter Schwarz, Konrad Adenauer – A German Politician and Statesman, vol. 2, Berghahn Books, Oxford, 1997, p. 34. Charlie Jeffrey, Simon Bulmer and William E. Paterson, Germany's European Diplomacy, Manchester University Press, Manchester, 2000, p. 55.
40. Fabrizio Saccomanni, conversation with author, Rome, 26 June 2007.
41. See Harold James, Making the European Monetary Union, Belknap Press, Cambridge, Mass., 2012.
42. Danièle Nouy, interview, Welt am Sonntag, 7 June 2015.
43. Jean Pisani-Ferry, André Sapir and Guntram Wolff, EU-IMF Assistance to Euro-Area Countries: An early assessment, Bruegel, Brussels, 2013, available at: http://www.bruegel.org/publications/publication-detail/publication/779-eu-imf-assistance-to-euro-area-countries-an-early-assessment/
44. International Monetary Fund, Greece: Ex post evaluation of exceptional access under the 2010 stand-by arrangement, IMF Country Report No. 13/156, June 2013, available at: http://www.imf.org/external/pubs/ft/scr/2013/cr13156.pdf
45. Lord (Gus) O'Donnell, speech, Vienna, 19 October 2015.
46. This new framework for European cooperation was proposed by a former UK foreign secretary, David Owen, in his book Europe Restructured: The Eurozone crisis and its aftermath, Methuen, York, 2012.
47. Nigel Lawson, comment to author, June 2013.

Index

133